CONTENTS

GW00578115

INTRODUCTION

The battle for Kasserine Pass in February 1943 was the baptism of fire for the US Army in the European theater in World War II. The German offensive to capture the mountain passes at Kasserine was Rommel's last attempt to regain the strategic initiative in North Africa. In spite of the initial success of Operation *Sturmflut*, the offensive quickly faltered and the Axis forces remained trapped in Tunisia. The US forces regained their balance and kept the Germans at bay at El Guettar a few weeks later. The noose around Army Group Afrika quickly tightened as joint attacks by Montgomery's Eighth Army and Anderson's First Army gradually enveloped and overcame the Axis defenses in the spring of 1943. The US Army's enlarged and strengthened II Corps was shifted to the northern front against Bizerte. Hitler refused to evacuate the trapped German and Italian forces, and in early May 1943 the Axis sacrificed over a quarter of a million troops, comparable in size to those lost a few months earlier at Stalingrad. The focus of this book is the battles for the Kasserine-Faïd passes and the subsequent efforts by the US Army to recover from this defeat in the final phase of the Tunisian campaign.

THE STRATEGIC BACKGROUND

North Africa was a peripheral theater of operations for both Germany and the United States, but both were cajoled into military operations by their allies. In Germany's case, Italy made a bold gamble in 1940 to expand its African colonies, a venture that quickly went sour with a sound British rebuff. The embarrassing Italian defeat in Africa prompted Hitler to dispatch a small force led by Erwin Rommel that arrived in February 1941. The Deutsches Afrika Korps' (DAK) victories against the overextended British Eighth Army led to a steady trickle of reinforcements to Rommel, but never enough for a decisive edge. Hitler's attention was shifting eastward towards Russia.

Africa was important in British grand strategy because of Britain's imperial commitments in Africa, the Middle East, and India. The Mediterranean was the vital link to the Middle East, and the Suez Canal controlled access to the trade routes to India. Furthermore, Britain was primarily a naval power with an army too small to single-handedly challenge that of a major continental power such as Germany. Britain's traditional approach for more than a century had been a strategy of peripheral engagement, taking advantage of the strategic mobility of its fleet to wear down the enemy in secondary theaters until a coalition could be formed to directly confront an adversary on land. Once the threat of a direct German invasion of Britain had abated in late 1940,

LEFT **This M4A1 medium tank of the Co. I commander, Capt. G.W. Meade, was one of the few survivors of the destruction of Hightower's 3/1st Armored Regiment at Sidi bou Zid. It is seen here in Kasserine Pass on February 24, 1943. (NARA)**

US vehicles taking part in the Operation *Torch* landings were prominently marked with US flags in the hope that the French would hold their fire. This is an M7 105mm howitzer motor carriage, the standard US self-propelled artillery in Tunisia.

Britain built up its forces in Egypt with the aim of defeating the Axis forces in this theater. The campaign in North Africa remained at a stalemate through most of 1941 and early 1942 with the battle line shifting east and west whenever either side enjoyed temporary advantages in forces, supplies, and new equipment. However, following Germany's invasion of the Soviet Union in June 1941, the prospects for the Afrika Korps faded. Russia became the Wehrmacht's primary theater of operations, and by the summer of 1942, the balance of forces in North Africa was shifting decidedly in Britain's favor.

Hitler's declaration of war on the United States in December 1941 reinforced British strategic predilections, and Churchill set about trying to convince Roosevelt of the advantages of a Mediterranean strategy. This approach was not widely shared in the United States, and in particular the US Army Chief of Staff, Gen. George C. Marshall, strongly favored a commitment of Allied forces into France as early as possible, preferably in 1943. As it would transpire, the Allies were not ready for a major land campaign in France in 1943. In a series of conferences between senior Allied leaders, the British gradually convinced their American counterparts to participate in Mediterranean operations in 1942–43 as a means to keep the pressure on the Wehrmacht until a landing in France was possible. In addition, Stalin and the Soviet leadership were also advocating combat action by the western Allies since the Red Army had been bearing the brunt of German attacks for more than a year. Roosevelt and Marshall finally acceded to British pressure, but the US commitment to the Mediterranean theater was half-hearted.

OPERATION *TORCH*

The Anglo-American plan for new North African operations was codenamed Operation *Torch*. By late October 1942, the British Eighth Army had secured the strategic initiative in North Africa at the second battle of El Alamein. German and Italian forces were in headlong

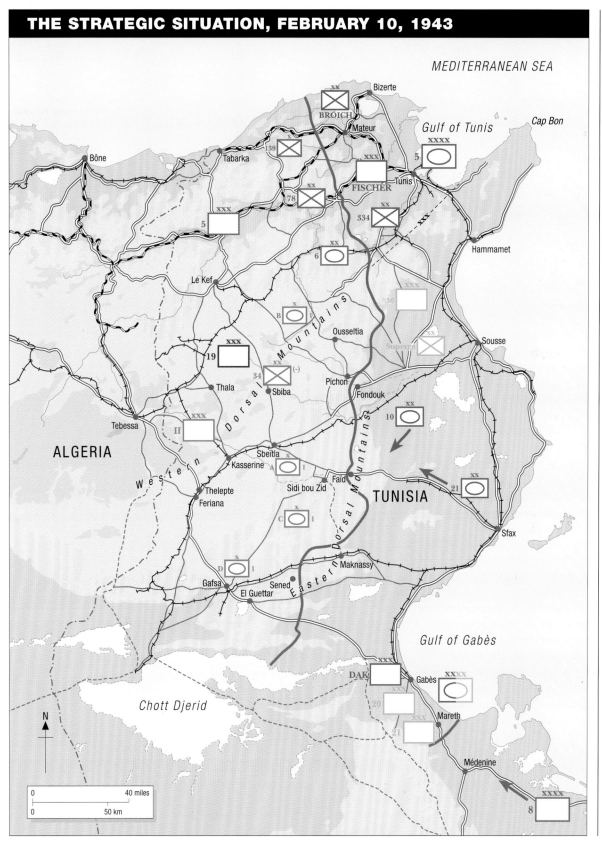

MEDITERRANEAN SEA

Bizerte

Gulf of Tunis

Cap Bon

BROICH

Mateur

Tabarka

139

5

Bône

78

FISCHER

Tunis

XXX

334

5

6

Hammamet

Le Kef

30

Ousseltia

B

Sousse

Superga

19

34 (-)

Pichon

Thala

Sbiba

Fondouk

Tebessa

II

10

Sbeïtla

Kasserine

A 1

Faïd

TUNISIA

21

ALGERIA

Sidi bou Zid

Western Dorsal Mountains

Dorsal Mountains

Eastern Dorsal Mountains

Thelepte
Feriana

C 1

Sfax

Gafsa

Sened
El Guettar

D 1

Maknassy

Chott Djerid

Gulf of Gabès

DAK

Gabès

20

XXXX

21

Mareth

Médenine

N

8

0   40 miles

0   50 km

retreat through Libya. The aim of Operation *Torch* was to squeeze the Axis forces out of North Africa from the other side. An Allied landing would be conducted at three locations in French North Africa by a primarily American force. The decision to rely on US forces in Operation *Torch* was due both to Britain's existing commitments in North Africa, as well as to the rancor between Britain and France in the aftermath of the 1940 French defeat. Not only had Britain evacuated its army from France in 1940 prior to the French surrender, but afterwards the Royal Navy attacked elements of the French Navy in Mers-el-Kebir harbor rather than permit major French warships to fall into German hands. The presumption was that American forces might not elicit the type of resistance that was likely to ensue if British forces were the most prominent element of the *Torch* landing force.

France's response to the forthcoming invasion of its North African colonies was in question. The Pétain government in France was careful to avoid antagonizing Germany for fear that Hitler would occupy the remainder of central and southern France, as well as the overseas colonies that were still under the control of the French Vichy government. Nevertheless, North Africa was a refuge for many military officers and officials who resented Pétain's collaboration with Germany since the 1940 armistice. The United States began dispatching secret agents to North Africa before the landings in the hope of convincing senior officials to side with the Allies. When the landings took place in November 1942, the French reaction was mixed. Although there was some resistance in a few

The race to seize Tunis was won by the Germans, who quickly deployed forces into the Tunisia bridgehead in December 1942, including this PzKpfw IV. (NARA)

locations, by and large the landings took place without serious opposition.

Hitler's reaction to the Allied landings was predictable: the remainder of France was occupied by the Wehrmacht, and Pétain was dismissed. This left the situation in the French colonies such as Tunisia and Algeria in doubt. With Rommel's star in the decline after the defeat at El Alamein, Hitler dispatched a second German contingent under Gen. Nehring to occupy the Tunisian bridgehead. A race developed to see who would seize Tunisia first—Anderson's First Army, marching from Algeria, or the 5th Panzer Army, arriving in Tunisia by aircraft and ship from Italy. The Germans won the race, and by mid December, a stalemate had developed along the Tunisian frontier with the Allies still too weak to overcome the Wehrmacht defenses, and the German forces too poorly supplied to drive the Allies back into Algeria. The winter weather was so cold and wet that the Allies presumed a major offensive would wait until spring.

The other ingredient in this volatile mix was the clash between the Eighth Army and Rommel's Panzerarmee Afrika retreating through Libya. Mussolini pleaded with Hitler to make a stand in Libya lest he lose face in yet another military disaster for the hapless Italian army. Rommel bluntly warned the high command that unless he was provided with reinforcements and supplies, he would have no choice but to retreat to more defensible ground across the Tunisian frontier. Rommel was out of favor with Hitler and was warned that supplies would not be forthcoming. Disregarding instructions that he stage a last ditch defense of Libya, he managed to extricate most of the German units and some

French forces in North Africa were equipped with obsolete equipment, such as this White-Laffly 50 AM armored car of the 2ᵉ Régiment de Chasseurs d'Afrique. This vehicle was knocked out by a 37mm gun in fighting with the US 26th Infantry near El Ancor west of Oran on November 8, 1942 shortly after the beginning of Operation *Torch*. This unit later fought alongside US and British troops in the defense of Thala on February 23, 1943 during the Kasserine Pass fighting. (MHI)

of the better Italian units into Tunisia by February 1943, shielded behind the French-built Mareth Line.

With Rommel's forces on the verge of joining 5th Panzer Army in Tunisia, Hitler and Mussolini began to make plans for the defense of the Tunisian bridgehead. A reorganization of command was planned, with Rommel ordered back to Germany to recuperate from exhaustion and health problems and his command being turned over to an Italian commander, Gen. Giovanni Messe. Panzerarmee Afrika would become the 1st Italian Army. However, Rommel saw one last tactical opportunity before he returned to Germany. The Allied defenses in Tunisia were still weak, and the southern flank was held by inexperienced American forces. Rommel dismissed the inexperienced US Army as "Britain's Italians" and believed that a hard blow would easily puncture the American lines. German Panzer forces could use the opportunity to race into Algeria, threatening Anderson's First Army. Rommel chose one last offensive to redeem his reputation, now in tatters after months of retreat.

The terrain in central Tunisia comprised flat, rocky desert interrupted by the rugged Dorsal Mountains.

CHRONOLOGY

1942

November 8 US troops land at three locations in French North Africa at the start of Operation *Torch*.

Mid December Germans deploy forces in northern Tunisia from Sicily and Italy, winning the race to seize Tunis.

1943

January 20 Rommel orders retreat of the German–Italian Panzer Army from Libya into Tunisia.

January 30 Arnim's 5th Panzer Army takes Faïd Pass from French garrison.

February 11 The Italian Comando Supremo (High Command) issues instructions for offensive in Tunisia by Rommel and Arnim.

February 14 Operation *Frühlingswind* begins with attack on CCA/1st Armored Division at Sidi bou Zid.

February 15 US counterattack at Sidi bou Zid is crushed; CCA withdraws to Sbeïtla.

February 16 Operation *Morgenluft* begins with occupation of Gafsa against little opposition.

February 17 US withdraws from Sbeïtla under pressure from 5th Panzer Army.

February 18 Reconnaissance elements of Rommel's battlegroup and Arnim's forces meet at Kasserine.

Midnight, February 18 The Comando Supremo authorizes Operation *Sturmflut* with Rommel in command.

February 19 Kampfgruppe DAK begins the assault against US defenses in Kasserine Pass and against combined US and British defenses near Sbiba; the attacks fail.

February 20 Attacks in Kasserine Pass finally overcome the defenses by evening.

February 21 The advance along the road to Tebessa is halted by CCB/1st Armored Division; 10th Panzer Division fights a bloody, day-long battle against stiff British defenses on the approach to Thala.

February 22 The German attack along the Tebessa road goes awry; the attack on Thala is halted by artillery; retreat is ordered at 1415 hours.

February 25 Allied forces reoccupy Kasserine Pass.

March 17 1st Infantry Division occupies Gafsa at start of Operation *Wop*.

March 23 10th Panzer Division attempts to stop American advance against the flank of the Mareth Line by an attack on El Guettar, which is repulsed with heavy losses.

April 10 German forces succeed in holding Fondouk and Pichon passes long enough to permit evacuation from Chott Position.

April 23 US II Corps launches an offensive in northern Tunisia towards Bizerte.

April 30 34th Division finally takes Hill 609, the major obstacle on the way to Mateur.

May 7 9th Infantry Division enters Bizerte; the city is captured the following day.

May 9 1st Armored Division reaches the Mediterranean; 5th Panzer Army surrenders at 1250 hours.

May 13 Remaining German forces in Tunisia surrender to the 18th Army Group.

OPPOSING COMMANDERS

AXIS COMMANDERS

Nominally, all Axis forces in North Africa were under the direction of the Italian Comando Supremo and its chief, Marshal Ugo Cavallero. The Comando Supremo was represented in the North African theater by the governor-general of Libya, Marshal Ettore Bastico. Bastico had a distinguished combat career, fighting in the campaign in Ethiopia and commanding the Italian CTV (Corps of Volunteer Troops) during the Spanish Civil War in 1937. Yet he had no more success than his predecessors in exercising control over his erstwhile subordinate, Erwin Rommel. German commanders held their Italian counterparts in contempt for their earlier failures in North Africa and Greece, and it was Rommel who largely set the operational agenda, not Bastico. He was damned by faint praise in later German memoirs, Rommel's chief of staff mockingly noting that Bastico gave Rommel "wide freedom of action."

The most visible Axis commander in North Africa was Erwin Rommel, whose early desert victories led Hitler to elevate him to Field Marshal status on June 22, 1942. Rommel's original command in North Africa in early 1941 was called the Deutsches Afrika Korps (DAK); in August 1941 his command was enlarged to Panzergruppe Afrika, with control of both the DAK and the Italian XX Corps. While the African campaign has attracted a great deal of attention in English-language histories of the war, it was a minor theater for the Wehrmacht, which was embroiled in a titanic struggle with the Red Army. Rommel was not regarded as highly by other German officers as by his Allied opponents; Prussian officers like von Arnim regarded him as an upstart not smart enough to have trained at the Kriegsakademie and who owed his lofty rank solely to Hitler's favor. Rommel's hard campaigns in 1941–42 took their toll and by the late summer of 1942 he was physically exhausted and suffering from medical problems. He left for Germany to recuperate on September 22, 1942, and handed over command to an Eastern Front veteran, Gen. Georg Stumme. Rommel's convalescence was brief, as Stumme died of a heart attack shortly after Montgomery launched the offensive at El Alamein on October 23, 1942. Hitler personally telephoned Rommel to ask him to return to Africa in hope of redeeming the looming disaster, and he arrived in early November 1942.

As German forces increased in the Mediterranean in late 1941, the Wehrmacht established the Oberbefehlshaber Süd (Commander-in-Chief South) at Frascati near Rome under Generalfeldmarschall Albert Kesselring in December 1941. Kesselring was a Luftwaffe officer and in addition to his role as OB-Süd, he commanded Luftflotte 2, the Luftwaffe force covering the Mediterranean. Kesselring was nominally under the

Feldmarschall Erwin Rommel's star was on the wane in January 1943 after the defeat at El Alamein and the precipitous retreat through Libya to the Tunisian frontier. (MHI)

Rommel's rival in Tunisia was General der Panzertruppen Hans-Jürgen von Arnim, commander of the 5th Panzer Army. (NARA)

Lt. Gen. Kenneth A.N. Anderson commanded the British First Army in northern Tunisia. (NARA)

command of Mussolini himself, and served as the air commander to the Comando Supremo. Kesselring had begun his military career in the Bavarian artillery, being elevated to the general staff in the winter of 1917 as a result of his demonstrated talent. He remained in the Reichswehr in the 1930s, until 1933 when he was ordered to become chief administrator of the Air Ministry in civilian dress. His primary responsibility was the creation of the infrastructure of the new Luftwaffe, and attracted the favorable attention of the Luftwaffe head, Hermann Göring. By the time war broke out, he had returned to uniform as commander of Luftflotte 1, the tactical close-support bomber and Stuka force that played such a prominent role in the 1939 campaign against Poland, and later as commander of Luftflotte 2 during the 1940 campaign against France. Kesselring's command relationship with the Italians and with Rommel was awkward and depended on his considerable political skills. Cavallero took Kesselring's appointment as a personal slight and so relations were strained from the start. Kesselring was nicknamed "Smiling Albert" for his charm, and he managed to foster good relations with the Italian senior commanders by tact and patience. Relations with the Italians deteriorated again in February when Cavallero was replaced by Gen. Vittorio Ambrosio, who exhibited "an unfriendly, even hostile attitude" according to Kesselring.

Rommel later wrote; "it is sometimes a misfortune to enjoy a certain military reputation. One knows one's own limits, but other people expect miracles." When Rommel failed to create more miracles with his increasingly emaciated and weary Afrika Korps in the summer of 1942, he fell out of favor with Hitler. When he returned in November 1942 after the El Alamein defeat, his messages back to Berlin were no longer the pugnacious promises of 1941 but pessimistic predictions of doom. Mussolini complained bitterly to Hitler about Rommel's precipitous retreat through Libya. The defense of Tunisia was being led by Gen. Walter Nehring and his improvised 90th Corps, but senior German commanders including Kesselring thought him even more pessimistic than Rommel. Kesselring pushed for a Panzer army to reinforce the Tunisian bridgehead, and Hitler agreed. Disappointed by Rommel's defeats and pessimism, Hitler's new favorite was General der Panzertruppen Hans-Jürgen von Arnim. Arnim commanded the new 17th Panzer Division and was seriously wounded in the initial invasion of the Soviet Union in June 1941. He returned to his command in September, taking part in the final stages of the Kiev encirclement. His performance was exemplary and he was sent to head the 39th Panzer Corps in November 1941 during the difficult fighting on the northern front. His reputation was further enhanced in May 1942 when he planned and led the attack to free the encircled German forces in the Kholm pocket. This attracted Hitler's attention, and in November 1942 when plans began to dispatch 5th Panzer Army to Tunisia to counter Operation *Torch*, Arnim was selected.

ALLIED COMMANDERS

The Allies enjoyed a more unified command structure than the Axis but had their share of difficulties as they adjusted to the new realities of coalition warfare. Both British and American leaders concluded that greater unity of command was required than had been the case during World War I, and in January 1942 the Combined Chiefs of Staff was formed to coordinate planning at the strategic level. Allied cooperation was inherently sounder than in the German–Italian case, as the two partners were far more equal in military capabilities. Although the United States had greater resources, Britain in 1942 had far more combat experience, giving British opinions on strategic and operational issues great weight. The Anglo-American relationship was better at the strategic command level than in the field, with British tactical commanders often being dismissive of the green and callow American forces.

In late February, Allied ground forces in North Africa were consolidated under the 18th Army Group headquarters, commanded by Gen. Harold Alexander, to the left, seen talking with Gen. Dwight Eisenhower and Gen. George S. Patton during a meeting at Feriana on March 17, 1943. (NARA)

Unity of command extended to theater command, and Gen. Dwight Eisenhower was selected as supreme commander for the Mediterranean Theater. Eisenhower had been appointed as commander of US forces in Europe in June 1942 by his mentor, US Army chief of staff Gen. George C. Marshall. Eisenhower was a quintessential staff officer, not a field commander. He had spent World War I training the infant US tank force while another young officer, George S. Patton, commanded the first US tank battalions in combat in France in 1918. Eisenhower had served ably as the aide to the flamboyant Gen. Douglas MacArthur in the Philippines in the 1930s, an invaluable exercise in the politics of command. After a stint as chief-of-staff of the Third Army in 1941, Eisenhower was recalled to Washington following Pearl Harbor on account of his experience in the Philippines. He greatly impressed Marshall and became the unofficial planner of American strategy in 1942. When the need for an overall US commander in Europe became evident in the summer of 1942, Eisenhower was Marshall's immediate choice even though he was still a very junior officer in rank and seniority. Eisenhower was appointed to head the Allied Expeditionary Force in North Africa by default. Marshall had continued to resist Churchill's plans for Operation *Torch*, and when the US side finally acceded in July 1942, command of the operation was offered to the American side as a political concession. Eisenhower was the obvious choice since he was already the commander of US forces in Europe, and had also won Churchill's trust. Eisenhower had a confident, extroverted personality, and was comfortable working with other ambitious and talented commanders. This was an essential ingredient in what was an intensely political command.

Maj. Gen. Lloyd Fredendall commanded the Center Task Force during Operation *Torch*, and subsequently Task Force Satin and the US II Corps. (NARA)

The US II Corps, known originally as Satin Force, was subordinated to the British First Army on January 21, 1943, under the command of Lt. Gen. Kenneth A.N. Anderson. He had won the Military Cross in World War I and served in the colonies in the interwar years. Anderson led the 11th Infantry Brigade in the Battle of France in 1940, and subsequently served as the acting commander of the 3rd Infantry Division. After Dunkirk, he commanded the 1st Infantry Division, rising to corps command in the spring of 1941. His American subordinates found him

Maj. Gen. Orlando "Pink" Ward, commander of the 1st Armored Division.

Col. Paul Robinett, the controversial but highly effective commander of Combat Command B, 1st Armored Division, seen here in a photo from a decade before the war. (MHI)

RIGHT Patton sped around the battlefield in this specially modified M3A1 scout car, seen here in Tunisia in March 1943 still wearing the insignia of his previous command, the I Armored Corps. (NARA)

" a dour and reticent Scotsman", and relations were proper but difficult. Command relationships were not helped by the differences between British and American command style. British commanders typically paid much closer attention to the tactical plans of their subordinates; the American command style was to make clear the objective of the mission and leave it to the discretion of the subordinate commander to work out the precise details. When the British style met the American style in Tunisia, the Americans felt that the British commanders were interfering because of doubts about their capabilities.

Command of the two US corps went to officers older than Eisenhower. Maj. Gen. Lloyd Fredendall led the Center Task Force that landed in Oran, and subsequently headed the Satin Force, the principal American combat element in Tunisia. Fredendall served as a staff officer in France in 1917–18, was appointed a colonel in 1935 after a posting with the inspector general, and in October 1940 became commander of the 4th Infantry Division. He was highly rated for his training skills and appointed to command II Corps in 1941 in time to take part in the Carolina maneuvers. Many American officers viewed him as one of the Army's shining stars, but British officers felt that he epitomized some of the less pleasant American traits—a loud, brassy know-it-all without the experience to justify his self-confidence. Fredendall's command style was marred by a tendency to use "tough-guy" slang, often leaving his subordinates in doubt about his precise intentions. For most of early 1943, his force had only a single complete division under his command, the 1st Armored Division, and he often circumvented the divisional commander, Maj. Gen. Orlando Ward, by issuing instructions directly to the division's combat commands. As a result, relations with Ward were extremely poor, and were further exacerbated by Fredendall's tendency to strip Ward of any tactical freedom by issuing very detailed instructions about the tactical disposition of his troops.

The other American commander in North Africa was Maj. Gen. George S. Patton, who led the Western Task Force that landed at

Casablanca and subsequently the I Armored Corps stationed in Morocco. Patton shared Fredendall's reputation as a colorful commander. He was an eccentric but passionate professional. Patton commanded the only large US tank unit in France in 1918, but returned to his beloved horse cavalry after the war when tanks proved to be a career dead-end. Patton was no fool, and when it became evident that the day of the horse cavalry had passed in the late 1930s, he transferred his considerable enthusiasm to the new armored force, becoming the commander of the new 2d Armored Division in January 1941. The I Armored Corps in Morocco included the 2d Armored Division and a number of separate tank battalions. The corps was left far from the battlefront, in part because of the lack of logistics to support it in Tunisia, and in part because of the need to retain a strategic reserve opposite Gibraltar and Spanish Morocco in case Germany forged an alliance, voluntary or otherwise, with Spain in the wake of occupying the rest of France. There was some concern that Hitler would push his forces along the Spanish coast and then into Spanish Morocco behind Allied lines as a bold counter to the Allied landings in North Africa. Patton's force was a counterweight to such an adventure.

Eisenhower brought in fellow West Point classmate Omar Bradley as an aide, but the need for new leaders after Kasserine saw Bradley appointed first as Patton's II Corps aide and then as II Corps' commander in the final month of the fighting. (MHI)

While Anglo-American relations were sometimes testy, relations with the French Army in North Africa were uncomfortable. When the French government in North Africa decided to side with the Allies, command of the French North African garrison went to Gen. Henri Giraud. The French had not forgiven the British for 1940 and Giraud refused to subordinate his forces to Anderson's First Army command. He did acknowledge the subordination of French forces to Eisenhower's Supreme Allied Command so, an expedient command structure was created with Eisenhower appointing Maj. Gen. Lucian Truscott as his deputy chief of staff for Tunisian operations at a forward command post at Constantine, with French forces reporting to Truscott rather than Anderson, and Truscott coordinating operations with Anderson. It was an unfortunate complication, calmed by the more cooperative attitude of Gen. Alphonse Juin, the French commander in Tunisia. Juin was a tough colonial veteran respected by American commanders. During the Tunisian command, Juin was primarily responsible for rebuilding the French army in North Africa for future commitment in Italy and France in 1944. As a result, Gen. Louise-Marie Koeltz commanded the French 19th Corps in Tunisia, which was positioned between Anderson's First Army and Fredendall's II Corps.

OPPOSING FORCES

AXIS FORCES

The Axis forces in Tunisia in January 1943 consisted of two distinct parts: Arnim's 5th Panzer Army in the Tunisian bridgehead, and Rommel's retreating Panzerarmee Afrika. Of the two forces, Arnim's was the more potent, having arrived more recently and thus being fresh and better equipped. Rommel's forces were worn down due to prolonged combat and exhaustion and had been starved of supplies, since priority had been given to Arnim's units.

The 5th Panzer Army consisted of two corps: Korpsgruppe Fischer, controlling the German elements of the army, and the Italian XXX Corps, controlling the Italian formations. Division von Broich, also sometimes known as the Schutzen Brigade von Broich, was an improvised unit formed of Luftwaffe paratroopers, the Italian 10th Bersaglieri Regiment, and various other German units that formed the core of the original Axis units airlifted into Tunisia in November 1942. The 334th Infantry Division was a new formation formed at the end of November 1942, and was somewhat understrength when deployed to Tunisia. The 10th Panzer Division was an experienced division that had served in France in 1940 and in Russia in 1941–42. Besides its usual Panzer regiments, it had the s.Pz.Abt. 501 Tiger battalion attached to it as the third battalion of Panzer Regiment 7. The 21st Panzer Division was shifted to 5th Panzer Army control in late January prior to the Kasserine Pass battles to shield Sfax while it was brought back up to strength. Its tanks were transferred to the 15th Panzer Division and replaced by the new Grün Panzer Battalion created in Tunis and Panzer Abteilung 190 formerly of the 90th Light Division. The Italian Superga

The workhorse of the Panzer units in North Africa was the PzKpfw III medium tank. This is one of the later PzKpfw III Ausf. Ls with the highly effective, long 50mm gun, which served with the 6th Company, Panzer Regiment 7 of the 10th Panzer Division at Kasserine Pass.

One of the most effective anti-tank weapons in Afrika Korps service was the 76.2mm PaK 36(r), a Soviet divisional gun captured in 1941 and put into use as an anti-tank gun. This example was knocked out by an M4 tank of 2/13th Armored on March 17 during the advance on Sened Station. (NARA)

Among the new weapons to debut in Tunisia was the 75mm PaK 40 anti-tank gun, a much more effective weapon than the inadequate 37mm gun in US Army use. This example was captured near Gafsa in early February 1943. (MHI)

Division had participated in the 1940 campaign against France and had subsequently been organized as an amphibious assault division. In late January, Arnim's forces in the Tunisian bridgehead numbered about 74,000 German and 26,000 Italian troops.

Rommel's Panzerarmee Afrika, renamed the German–Italian Panzer Army (Deutsche–Italienische Panzerarmee, or DIP) late in the Libyan campaign, had a paper strength greater than Arnim's force, but in reality it was smaller due to the heavy loss of forces since the defeat at El Alamein and the retreat through Libya. German units totaled about 30,000 troops but the divisions were badly understrength and tended to operate as improvised *kampfgruppen* (battlegroups). The Italian elements of the army were the 131st Centauro Armored Division, four infantry divisions, and the Saharan Group numbering about 48,000 troops in mid January. The Centauro armored division was one of the best Italian armored divisions, and had participated in the campaigns in the Balkans, prior to being sent to Africa to take part in the Libyan campaign. By the time of the Tunisian campaign, it had been reduced in strength to barely a battalion of tanks. Rommel had only about 130 German and Italian tanks of which less than 60 were fully operational, and half of which were the obsolete Italian types.

When Rommel ordered the retreat from the Tarhuna-Homs defenses on the night of January 19/20 and the establishment of a temporary

The most famous weapon in the German anti-tank arsenal was the formidable 88mm Flak gun, frequently used in the improvised anti-tank role due to its extremely effective long-range firepower. (MHI)

Heavy fire support was provided by the 150mm sFH 18, the standard Wehrmacht heavy field howitzer. (MHI)

headquarters at Sfax, the stage had been set for the joining of the two main Axis forces in North Africa in the Tunisian bridgehead. As the two Axis armies began to connect, some of Rommel's better units were transferred to Arnim in central Tunisia in hope of rebuilding them away from the front lines. Arnim's intended force was not yet complete, with units waiting in Sicily, Italy and elsewhere while transport was assembled. Hitler planned to raise German strength in the Tunisian bridgehead to 140,000 troops, but the Stalingrad operations taking place at the same time put a distinct limit on reinforcements to North Africa.

After the heavy losses in Libya, Italian troops made up the minority of Axis forces in Tunisia. The Italian army displayed all the problems typical of those of an impoverished nation. The standard Italian tank, the M14/41, was a light tank with thin armor and an inadequate gun. Italian artillery was adequate if antiquated, but its anti-tank arsenal was based around the obsolete 47mm gun, which was ineffective against contemporary Allied tanks. Kesselring complained that the Italian armed forces were more trained for display than for action. Italian infantry training was old-fashioned, unrealistic, and based on outdated tactical doctrine. Enlisted–officer relations were feudal and there was little of the

Italian artillery in Tunisia was adequate but somewhat antiquated, as is suggested by this Cannone da 104/32 mod. 15, which was a Skoda design captured from the Austro-Hungarian army in World War I. About 35 were in use with the XXX Corps in Tunisia in 1943. (NARA)

One of the innovations seen in Tunisia was the new 150mm Nebelwerfer 41, which was soon dubbed the "Screaming Meemie" by US troops due to its frightening sound. (MHI)

sense of comradeship and shared mission that was the fabric of the German military ethos. Some Italian units were much better than average, and the Italian tank units were so well regarded by the Germans that in Tunisia they were subordinated to a German corps instead of reinforcing the beleaguered Italian infantry corps. Specialized Italian formations such as the Bersaglieri, and the Young Fascists (*Giovani Fascisti*) were also good. The Italian army continued to improve due to war experiences, better training and improved tactics. Italian weaponry remained a debilitating problem, thanks to their shortsighted German allies. Instead of assisting in Italian re-equipment using the extensive arsenal captured from the Red Army in 1941 or through licensed production of better German weapons designs, the Wehrmacht continued to ignore Italian shortcomings to their own peril. The performance of Italian troops in Tunisia was undoubtedly far better than in Egypt in 1940 or in the Libyan campaign of 1941, but the Italian army remained a weak link in the Axis coalition.

Due to heavy troop commitments in Russia, the German units deployed to Africa favored weapons over manpower. A disproportionate share of the German units in Tunisia were elite Panzer, motorized

The principal Italian anti-tank weapon was the 47mm gun, which was obsolete by 1943 standards—though not much worse than the US 37mm gun. (MHI)

One of the more curious Italian vehicles used in Tunisia was the Mototricolo Guzzi 500 Trialce, which was used to carry supplies. These are seen near a field kitchen in Tunisia, bringing food to the frontline troops. (MHI)

infantry or Luftwaffe units. German tanks in 1943 were on a par with Allied tanks, with a decided shift towards the long-barreled gun versions of the PzKpfw III and PzKpfw IV. Tunisia also saw the combat debut of several new weapons in the west including the Tiger heavy tank, the Nebelwerfer multiple rocket launcher, and the PaK 40 75mm anti-tank gun. The German units in Tunisia were for the most part combat experienced, battle-hardened units, at a time when the Wehrmacht was at the peak of its combat effectiveness.

The reconstitution of Rommel's bedraggled forces in Tunisia depended in large measure on the ability of the Axis powers to supply the Tunisian bridgehead across the Mediterranean. Arnim originally estimated supply demands at about 50,000 tons monthly, later revised to 60,000 tons. Seaborne transport at the end of 1942 consisted of about 40 merchant ships, supplemented by 20 Siebel naval ferries, and some French shipping from southern France that had been seized in November 1942. The sea lanes were hotly contested by British submarines and aircraft, and in

December 1942, 26 Axis ships were sunk and 9 damaged of the 127 supply missions undertaken. In desperation, the Axis began to use a wider range of vessels including more ferries, small coastal vessels, and even French river barges. To avoid the hazards of seaborne transport, the Luftwaffe reorganized their air transport forces in the Mediterranean theater. On average about 200 Ju-52 tri-motor transports and 15 of the enormous Me-323 Gigant transports were available, providing an additional 585 tons per day from bases in Sicily and southern Italy. During the reinforcement of the Tunisian bridgehead between November 1942 and January 1943, a total of 81,222 German and 30,735 Italian troops were shipped to Tunisia and 100,594 tons of supplies delivered, including 428 tanks, 5,688 vehicles and 729 artillery pieces. January 1943 was the peak month of deliveries, reaching 36,326 tons, of which about 15 percent was air-delivered. The total began to decline due to Allied counter-action, falling steadily to 23,017 tons in April—less than half of the Axis requirements.

One of the few German advantages in the Tunisian theater was in air support. This was due in large measure to the proximity of an extensive network of airbases and support facilities in Sicily and southern Italy. While neither the Axis nor Allies could claim air superiority over Tunisia, the balance in the air was in favor of the Axis through March 1943.

Axis order of battle, Tunisia, late January 1943

5TH PANZER ARMY	**General der Panzertruppen Hans-Jürgen von Arnim**
21st Panzer Division	Generalleutnant Hans-Georg Hildebrandt
Korpsgruppe Fischer	**Generalmajor Wolfgang Fischer**
10th Panzer Division	Generalmajor Wolfgang Fischer
334th Infantry Division	Generalleutnant Friedrich Weber
Division von Broich	Col. Friedrich Freiherr von Broich
5th Fallschirmjäger Regiment	
XXX Corps	**Generale di Corpo d'Armata Vittorio Sogno**
1st Superga Division	Gen. di Divisione Dante Lorenzelli
47th Grenadier Regiment	Lt. Col. Buse
50th Special Brigade	Gen. di Brigata Giovanni Imperiali di Francavilla
GERMAN-ITALIAN PANZER ARMY	**Generalfeldmarschall Erwin Rommel**
Deutsches Afrika Korps	**Generaleutnant Hans Cramer**
15th Panzer Division	Generalmajor Willibald Borowietz
131st Centauro Armored Division	Gen. Giorgio Calvi di Bergolo
1st Luftwaffe Jäger Brigade	
XX Corps	**Gen. di Divisione Tadeo Orlando**
13th Young Fascists Infantry Division	Gen. di Divisione Nino Sozzani
101st Trieste Infantry Division	Gen. di Brigata Francesco La Ferla
90th Light Afrika Division	Generalmajor Teodor Graf von Sponeck
XXI Corps	**Gen. d'Armata Paolo Berardi**
16th Pistoia Infantry Division	Gen. di Brigata Giuseppe Falugi
80th La Spezia Infantry Division	Gen. di Brigata Gavino Pizzolato
164th Light Afrika Division	Generalmajor Kurt Freiherr von Liebenstein
Ragruppamento Sahariano	Gen. di Brigata Alberto Mannerini

Axis forces enjoyed the advantage of extensive airbases in Tunisia and Sicily to support ground operations in Tunisia. This is a Fw-190A fighter captured on one of the Bizerte airfields in May 1943. (MHI)

ALLIED FORCES

Allied forces in central Tunisia were in a process of flux through much of January 1943. The area was initially held by units of Juin's Détachement d'Armée Française (DAF). The Germans had disarmed most of the French forces in Tunisia in November 1942, so the French military presence in Tunisia had to be reconstituted from elsewhere in French North Africa. Juin assigned a "Covering Detachment" to the two Dorsal mountain ranges with the aim of covering the British right flank and preventing German entry into Algeria through the Tebessa area. The first French force deployed was Gen. G. Barré's CSTT (Commandement Supérieur des Troupes de Tunisie) which consisted of five battalions of infantry. It took part in the fighting against the Italian Superga Division in late December 1942. The CSTT was gradually reinforced as units were scraped together from Algeria and Morocco. These units eventually formed Gen. L. Koeltz's 19th Army Corps. Its principal element in January 1943 was the Division de Marche de Constantine (DMC) under Gen. Welvert, which was an improvised division assigned to defend the area around Constantine. Other French units were gradually fed into the Tunisian front as they became available. Besides the main units in central Tunisia, the southern desert flank was patrolled by Gen. Delay's Front Est Saharien, consisting of local troops and Foreign Legion detachments on horse, camel and light trucks. The French forces in Tunisia included tough local troops led by French officers, units recruited from the local French communities, and Foreign Legion units. Even in the best of times, these units were not well equipped by European standards since their main role was to defend the colonies from local insurrections. The armistice of 1940 put further constraints on their size and equipment, for example forbidding the deployment of anti-tank guns and restricting the quality and quantity of armored vehicles. As a result, the French forces in Tunisia were mostly light infantry forces with mediocre infantry weapons, poor support weapons, and obsolete armored vehicles. Although some of the individual units were quite good, they had not been trained to operate in conventional divisions. They were best when employed for patrolling or raids, but could not stand up to prolonged conventional campaigns. They were a third-rate army with a first-rate soul.

The first major US unit to take part in the Tunisian fighting was Combat Command B (CCB) of the 1st Armored Division, commanded in January 1943 by Col. Paul Robinett. The 1st Armored Division had three combat commands, which were battlegroups made up from constituent battalions for specific missions. Only CCB was deployed in November–December, since this was all that could be supported from the distant logistic bases in Algeria. After the relatively easy landings and the light fighting against the French, US troops in North Africa were cocky and optimistic. They were confident that they

were the best-trained and best-equipped troops in the world, and would kick the Germans out of Africa with little effort. Robinett's CCB was not so callow after a month of hard fighting in December 1942. They had quickly learned that US Army training was artificial and inadequate, doctrine and tactics were little more than wishful thinking, and the equipment was good for 1939 but not up to 1943 standards.

US armored divisions in early 1943 had two tank regiments and only a single mechanized infantry regiment, since their primary role was offensive exploitation. The 1st Armored Division was poorly suited to the defensive mission it was assigned in Tunisia since it was so short of infantry. As a result, portions of the 1st and 34th Infantry divisions were gradually fed into the II Corps lines as the logistics permitted. They were seldom committed at regimental level, but rather individual battalions were parceled out to 1st Armored Division task forces to reinforce their overextended defensive positions. Contrary to doctrine, the 1st Armored Division's three combat commands were widely dispersed to fill gaps along the excessive frontline and not used as a concentrated force. To make matters worse, a fourth combat command was created in January 1943, which further diluted its strength.

In spite of the tank losses in CCB from the November–December 1942 fighting, the division was nearly full strength in early February by stripping tanks out of the uncommitted 2d Armored Division and had a total of 85 M3 light tanks and 202 medium tanks in early February 1943. The division was lavishly equipped by German standards, but except for the combat-hardened CCB, the division was wholly inexperienced. This was all the more serious, as US tactical doctrine at the time had not undergone the test of war. US Army armored doctrine was peculiar in a number of respects. The lessons of the 1940 campaign in France had led to the creation of a special Tank Destroyer command, specifically earmarked for dealing with the Panzer threat. This force, a quasi-independent branch separate from the Armored Force and the Infantry, deployed its battalions under separate tank destroyer groups at corps or army level. The idea was to

Only the 2/13th Armored, 1st Armored Division was still using the obsolete M3 medium tank in Tunisia in February 1943, an example of which is shown here. However, following the heavy losses at Kasserine Pass, nearly half of the replacement medium tanks were of this type. (NARA)

The US infantry anti-tank companies in Tunisia were dependent on the obsolete 37mm anti-tank gun, which was ineffective against contemporary German Panzers in a frontal engagement. By this time, the British were using the 6-pdr (57mm) gun. (NARA)

Mines were widely employed by both sides in Tunisia. This US Army lieutenant is seen using a bayonet to probe for buried mines while the soldier next to him removes one. (NARA)

keep the tank destroyers in reserve until the Panzer attack materialized, then rush the battalions forward in a concentrated mass to defeat the enemy tanks. The doctrine was controversial and had not kept pace with tactical developments in Europe since being hastily formulated in 1940. The prominence given to tank destroyers was not shared by any other major army. To make matters worse, the battalions committed to Tunisia were still equipped with expedient tank destroyers, a 37mm gun bolted in the back of a ¾ ton truck, and World War I French 75mm guns mounted in half-tracks. The tank destroyer force distorted armored division doctrine as well. Since the tank destroyer force was supposed to deal with the Panzer threat, the armored divisions concentrated on a mechanized cavalry mission focused on their use as an exploitation force once breakthrough was achieved. Tank fighting was not a significant mission for the division and the 1942 Armored Force field manual on tactics devoted only two of its 450 pages to the subject of tank-vs.-tank combat. Doctrine shaped training and tactics, and the fighting in Tunisia would clearly demonstrate that both were contrived and unrealistic.

US equipment in Tunisia was of varied quality. Infantry equipment was generally excellent except for the 37mm anti-tank gun. The infantry did not want to be burdened by a heavier anti-tank gun, and even though the much better British 6-pdr was already being manufactured in the US for Lend-Lease, the infantry refused to accept it. This would prove to be a significant issue in the 1943 fighting. The 2.36in. "bazooka" rocket launcher was

Mortars, such as this US 81mm version, proved to be highly effective in the Tunisian mountain fighting. (NARA)

only entering service at the time of the Tunisia campaign and few troops had been trained to use it. Most of the medium tanks in the 1st Armored Division were the M4 and M4A1 medium tank, better known by its British name, the Sherman. It was widely regarded as one of the best tanks in the world at the time. Only one battalion, Gardiner's experienced 2/13th Armored in the CCB, still had some of the archaic M3 medium tanks. The M3 and M3A1 light tanks used by two light battalions were obsolete with thin armor and a 37mm gun that was hard-pressed to defeat German Panzers. US artillery was excellent from a technical standpoint, but unseasoned.

The US role in Tunisia expanded considerably in January. Arnim's 5th Panzer Army began contesting the French control of the Eastern Dorsal mountains in mid January 1943, and seized Pichon and Fondouk passes. After visiting the line, Gen. Anderson felt that the French were on the verge of collapse. He did not trust the French to hold his right flank, so he discussed reinforcing the American forces in Tunisia. Eisenhower agreed to consolidate the 1st Infantry Division, move the rest of the 34th Division from Algeria, and transfer the 9th Infantry Division from Morocco. Even as late as the first week of February, the 1st Infantry Division was scattered along a 200-mile front from Medjez el Bab in the north to Gafsa in the south with its 16th Infantry and headquarters to the French 19th Corps, the 18th Infantry to the British V Corps, and the 26th Infantry to CCB, 1st Armored Division in the Ousseltia Valley. Not only were the division's elements widely dispersed, their frontages were exceptionally thin. The one infantry regiment under divisional command, the 16th, was covering a line 22 miles long. As the 34th Division arrived, its units were deployed in similarly disjointed fashion. The 168th Infantry had been deployed near Constantine since January 11 to guard lines of communication, and on January 29 was

US artillery proved very effective in the later fighting in Tunisia where it was possible to concentrate divisional artillery. A key ingredient in artillery fire support was the forward observer team, such as the one shown here. (NARA)

The French colonial troops in Tunisia were poorly equipped, as is evident from this horse artillery seen near Pont-du-Fahs in February 1943. (MHI)

ABOVE **French units were gradually re-equipped with US weapons, such as this 105mm howitzer seen here on February 12, 1943 on the Tunisian front. (MHI)**

ABOVE, RIGHT **The French colonial units were recruited from the local French and Arab communities and led by French officers. These officers from a Goum unit were photographed in Bizerte on May 9, 1943. Their dress reflects their diverse traditions: the captain to the left in a spahi *gandourah* and French beret, the next officer in a classic woollen *djellbah* and local cap, the third officer in French Sahara uniform with the light blue *képi* of the Sahara companies, and the officer on the far right with a French *bonnet de police* and a captured Italian *saharienne* bush jacket. (NARA)**

shifted to the command of the 1st Armored Division in the Gafsa–Sbeïtla area. As two battalions of the 133d Infantry arrived, they were deployed to cover the Pinchon and Fondouk passes during the first half of February.

The French pointedly asked why the Americans couldn't move the idle 2d Armored Division from Morocco to Tunisia, but the weak logistical chain in the theater limited the size of the force that could be supported. The railroad line to Tebessa could provide only about a third of the daily requirements of the existing units in II Corps, and the rest had to come by truck. The trucks by now were wearing out after months of hard use, and a new supply of trucks from the US was not expected until the middle of February at the earliest. Logistics were the main reason that US forces in central Tunisia were so modest in size.

Eisenhower instructed Anderson and Fredendall to concentrate 1st Armored Division to serve as an operational reserve due to the extensive frontage in central Tunisia. This did not take place prior to the Faïd–Kasserine battles as not all of the US infantry had arrived yet. Anderson expected that the American sector would remain a relatively quiet theater while the main action occurred opposite British elements of the First Army in northern Tunisia, and along the Tunisian–Libyan frontier as Rommel's forces retreated before Montgomery's Eighth Army. As would soon become apparent, Rommel had other plans.

Allied forces, Central–Southern Tunisia, late January 1943

19ᵉ CORPS D'ARMÉE (French Army)	Gen. Louis-Marie Koeltz
Commandement Supérieur des Troupes de Tunisie	Gen. Georges Barré
Division de Marche de Constantine	Gen. Joseph E. Welvert

II Corps (US Army)	Maj. Gen. Lloyd Fredendall
1st Armored Division	Maj. Gen. Orlando Ward
1st Infantry Division	Maj. Gen. Terry Allen
34th Division	Maj. Gen. Russell Hartle

OPPOSING PLANS

The fighting in central Tunisia was dominated by its geography, and especially the mountains (locally called *djebels*). Immediately to the west of the coastal plain is the Eastern Dorsal chain stretching south from Tunis towards the Mareth Line. Transit through the steep mountains was through critical passes at Pinchon and Fondouk on the Sousse–Sbeïtla road, at Faïd on the Sfax–Sbeïtla road, and through Maknassy on the southern approaches. Behind the Eastern Dorsals lie the Western Dorsals, which eventually merge with the Atlas Mountains in neighboring Algeria. There were several critical passes through the Western Dorsals, including Kasserine, which provided access to the key Allied staging base in Algeria at Tebessa. All German offensive plans had to keep these geographical factors in mind. Initially, Kesselring wanted to establish a deep defensive line running from Bone on the Mediterranean coast, through Tebessa, to the impenetrable Chott Djerid salt marshes. Barring that possibility, he felt that a defensive line running down the eastern side of the Western Dorsals would be adequate. However, lacking sufficient forces in late 1942, the actual German defensive line in January 1943 was along the eastern side of the Eastern Dorsals, with no strategic depth. Axis forces were configured like a barbell, with the 5th Panzer Army in the north, the German–Italian Panzer Army in the south along the Mareth Line, and very few forces in the center. The greatest German vulnerability lay in this middle area, since a vigorous Allied attack could push to the sea near Sfax, isolating Arnim's and Rommel's forces. Up to January 1943, with the weak French forces occupying central Tunisia, there was not much of a threat. However, with larger American forces arriving, Kesselring and Arnim became increasingly concerned about an American drive along the Sfax corridor.

PRELIMINARY MOVES: FROM SENED STATION TO FAÏD PASS

The plans of both sides in February 1943 were heavily shaped by a series of raids and spoiling attacks conducted by both sides in the last days of January 1943. Kesselring and the Comando Supremo wanted Arnim to stage a major offensive, seizing Faïd Pass, occupying the Gafsa basin, and attacking the American supply base at Tebessa. Instead, on January 24, 1943 Arnim issued orders for a more limited spoiling attack, arguing that he did not have the resources to do more. His plan was restricted to a few small battlegroups of the 5th Panzer Army attacking the French garrisons in the Faïd area to prevent the Allies from staging an attack towards Sfax through these key passes. At roughly the same time, the US

II Corps commander, Gen. Fredendall, was considering a raid aimed at keeping the Germans off-balance until the corps could be built up enough to make a bolder strike. Combat Command C was ordered to attack Sened Station as a stepping stone for a later attack towards the key road junction at Maknassy.

The Americans struck first, and CCC took Sened with little resistance. Although the French commanders pleaded with Fredendall to reinforce the weak French forces holding the passes further north, Fredendall decided that a planned attack on Maknassy would indirectly protect the passes since it would attract German attention further south. This raid did not take place, as in the meantime Arnim had launched his attack on Faïd.

The Axis attack force comprised the 21st Panzer Division supported by Imperiale's 50th Special Brigade to occupy Faïd Pass once it was seized. The pass was held by a battalion of the French 2nd RTA (Régiment de Tirailleurs Africaine) while a battalion of the 3rd Zouaves held the nearby pass at Rebaou, four miles to the south. They were supported by 75mm guns and some anti-tank guns of the 67th RAA (Régiment d'Artillerie Algérien) and a platoon of obsolete World War I-vintage Renault FT tanks.

The attack against Faïd Pass by Kampfgruppe Pfeiffer began at 0400 hours on January 30, spearheaded by eight Italian Semovente assault guns. The initial attack was brought to a halt by French artillery after at least three of the Semovente had been knocked out. The more heavily equipped Kampfgruppe Grün, which included the tanks of 1./Pz.Rgt. 5, was able to push through the 3rd Zouaves in Rebaou Pass and then encircle Faïd Pass from the opposite side. By noon, the French 2nd RTA was trapped between the two German battlegroups.

When the attack began, the French divisional commander Gen. Welvert rushed to Sidi bou Zid and pleaded with Brig. Gen. Raymond McQuillin, the commander of CCA, 1st Armored Division to intervene. Because of the excessively rigid command structure, McQuillin radioed Fredendall who in turn bucked the request up the chain of command to Gen. Anderson, who responded around 0900 hours "to restore the situation at Faïd." Fredendall then instructed McQuillin to move on Faïd "without weakening his defenses of Sbeïtla," which he interpreted to mean to deal with the Faïd attack with a small task force as any substantial force would weaken Sbeïtla. He dispatched two reconnaissance detachments to Faïd and Rebaou, which reported back at noontime that, indeed, strong German forces were operating on either side of the Eastern Dorsals. McQuillin finally created two task forces led by Col. Alexander Stark and Col. William Kern using the 26th Infantry, 3/1st Armored, the 701st Tank Destroyer Battalion and supporting elements. TF Stark was sent to relieve Faïd Pass while TF Kern headed for Rebaou Pass. In addition, Combat Command C, which had been scheduled to assault Maknassy under the earlier scheme, was directed instead to Sidi bou Zid to await the outcome of the attack by the two small task forces, only to be told later in the day to return to the original scheme of raiding Maknassy. Amidst this confusion, the counterattack against Faïd and Rebaou passes on January 31 failed. The forces committed to the action were far too small and too late, and the Germans had set up good defenses including a battery of 88mm guns. Another attempt on February 1 was equally unsuccessful. To further exploit the situation, Arnim sent

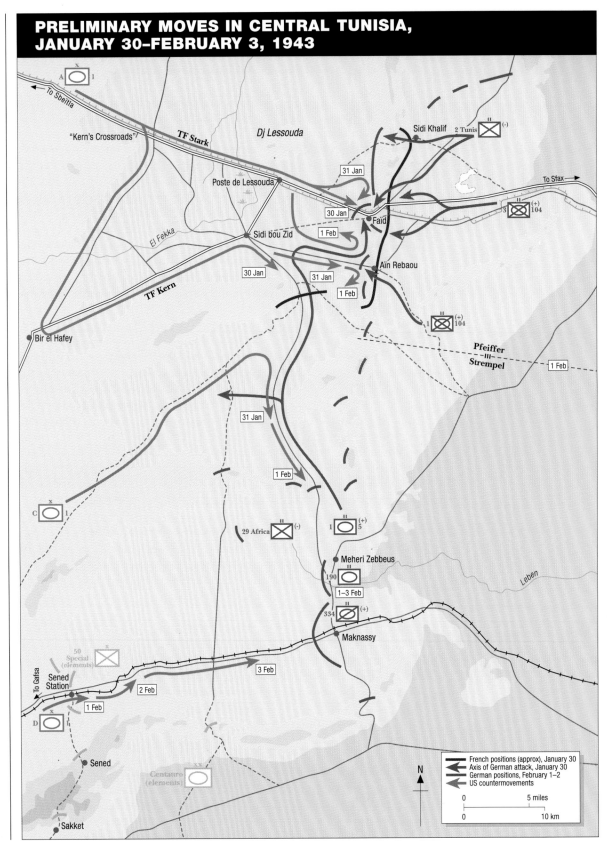

PRELIMINARY MOVES IN CENTRAL TUNISIA, JANUARY 30–FEBRUARY 3, 1943

A [X] 1

To Sbeitla

"Kern's Crossroads"

TF Stark

Dj Lessouda

Sidi Khalif   2 Tunis [XX] (-)

31 Jan

Poste de Lessouda

To Sfax

30 Jan

3 [XX] (+) 104

Faïd

Sidi bou Zid

1 Feb

El Fekka

30 Jan

Aïn Rebaou

TF Kern

31 Jan

1 Feb

1 [XX] (+) 104

Bir el Hafey

Pfeiffer
—III—
Strempel

1 Feb

31 Jan

1 Feb

C [X] 1

29 Africa [XX] (-)   1 [O] (+) 5

Meheri Zebbeus

190 [O]

1–3 Feb

334 [⌀] (+)

Maknassy

50
Special
(elements) [X]

To Gafsa

3 Feb

Sened
Station

2 Feb

1 Feb

D [O] 1

Sened

Centauro
(elements) [O]

N

French positions (approx), January 30
Axis of German attack, January 30
German positions, February 1–2
US countermovements

0   5 miles
0   10 km

Sakket

another *kampfgruppe* from the 10th Panzer Division to deal with the French garrison in the Pichon Pass further north on January 31. From Arnim's perspective, these actions provided a temporary relief from the threat of an Allied attack towards the Sfax corridor.

THE GERMAN PLAN

The outcome of the Faïd Pass clash set the stage for the ensuing Kasserine Pass fighting. The Faïd skirmishes convinced the German commanders that the Americans were inexperienced and badly dispersed. The weakly held American front was an opportunity, not a threat. With Faïd Pass effectively blocked, Arnim wanted to deal with the more pressing threat to 5th Panzer Army posed by the British First Army in northern Tunisia. To relieve pressure on Tunis, he wanted to strike towards the Fondouk Pass, threatening the British right flank and their connections with the French and Americans further south. This plan, codenamed Operation *Kuckucksei* (Cuckoo's Egg), was reviewed by the Comando Supremo during the first few days of February.

On January 31, Rommel's replacement, Gen. Messe, arrived at his headquarters, ready to take command. On the verge of being relieved, Rommel conceived a more ambitious operation than Arnim's as one last grasp for glory. After having been chased out of Libya by Montgomery's Eighth Army, Rommel's forces were establishing defensive positions along the Mareth Line. The situation on this front was relatively stable as the British had outrun their supplies and needed time to reestablish their logistical tail. German engineers had sabotaged Tripoli's dock facilities, and it would take weeks for Montgomery to build up supplies for another offensive. The front with the Eighth Army held no prospects for offensive adventures; the German–Italian Panzer Army was too weak to expect any dramatic gains from attacking Montgomery. Rommel needed additional forces to reinforce his attack and he needed a more vulnerable opponent. An attack against the inexperienced and thinly spread Americans served both purposes. Rommel was dismissive of the

The risky naval supply operations to Tunisia were supplemented by an intensive airlift campaign, and the Junkers Ju-52 formed the backbone of this effort. This damaged transport is seen on one of the airfields in the Bizerte area in May 1943. (MHI)

Americans after Faïd Pass, and he had little concern about the French colonial units.

Instead of merely blocking the passes through the Eastern Dorsals, as Arnim had done with the Faïd raid, Rommel wanted to continue west to the key passes through the Western Dorsals, such as Kasserine. Then, a German mechanized force could threaten to sweep into Algeria and destroy the Allied supply hub at Tebessa via Kasserine, or threaten to cut off the British First Army in northern Tunisia via Thala. Rommel probably recognized that the chances of such a dramatic outcome were slim, but an attack could at least give the green Americans a bloody nose and buy time to reinforce German defenses in the Tunisian bridgehead and along the Mareth Line. Rommel was never a commander to turn down a desperate but lucrative gamble, and he hoped he could leave North Africa with a victory as his swansong. To conduct such an attack, he would need more than his battered forces could provide. His plan was to employ the mobile elements of the German–Italian Panzer Army, while leaving the infantry units to hold the Mareth Line. But he also needed another Panzer battle group from Arnim's 5th Panzer Army, which required approval from Rome. On February 3, 1943 Rommel forwarded his attack plan to the Comando Supremo.

Gen. Ambrosio, the Italian chief of staff, was sympathetic to Rommel's plan, realizing that Mussolini's political fortunes had been threatened by the precipitous retreat of Axis forces from the Italian colony of Libya. A victory, even a tactical one, would help to calm the political crisis in Italy. Kesselring hoped that a striking victory in Africa would compensate for the final surrender of von Paulus's 6th Army at Stalingrad on February 2.

Kesselring met with Arnim and Rommel at Gabès on February 9 in the hope of reaching an agreement. Arnim argued that the German forces in Tunisia did not have the resources for Rommel's ambitious plans, and that his more limited offensive would serve both to constrain the Americans and threaten the British First Army. After discussing the issue with Kesselring, Ambrosio proposed a compromise on February 11. Instead of a unified attack directed by Rommel, two complementary attacks would be conducted separately by Arnim and Rommel. Arnim would exploit his Faïd Pass success with Operation *Frühlingswind* (Spring

Wind) surging out of Faïd towards Sidi bou Zid, and destroying CCA of the 1st Armored Division. Rommel would launch the second spoiling attack, dubbed Operation *Morgenluft* (Morning Breeze) that would take Gafsa, 60 miles to the south, thereby ending any threat to the rear of the Mareth defenses. Rommel's forces were too weak to conduct such an attack without reinforcements, so Arnim's 5th Panzer Army would launch the attack, and then transfer the 21st Panzer Division back to Rommel to reinforce his operations. Ambrosio and Kesselring left open the issue of a further advance into the Western Dorsals until the first phase of the attacks had been undertaken. The precise date of *Frühlingswind* was left to Arnim, as the cold, rainy winter weather in early February had been turning the battlefield to mud, inhibiting a Panzer advance.

ALLIED PLANS

Eisenhower's initial plan for the employment of II Corps was dubbed Operation *Satin*, scheduled for January 22, 1943. This would consist of a mobile raid by 1st Armored Division towards Sfax, Gabès or Kairouan intended to disrupt Rommel's supply lines from northern Tunisia. This was the Germans' primary concern, but US forces in central Tunisia were too weak and too inexperienced to carry it out. Senior British commanders were very skeptical of such a risky venture and Eisenhower dropped it on their advice. Instead, at a commanders' conference in mid January he indicated that II Corps operations would be primarily defensive in orientation and on January 20 he reaffirmed this by instructing Fredendall that the 1st Armored Division was to remain as a mobile reserve. The German capture of Faïd Pass only reinforced Eisenhower's view that this sector should remain dormant until the anticipated spring offensive.

From Anderson's perspective, the II Corps and the central Tunisian front were secondary concerns. His main focus was on the British corps of his First Army and their goal of stamping out Arnim's 5th Panzer Army in the north around Tunis. He realized that once the winter weather abated, Montgomery's Eighth Army would confront Rommel along the Mareth Line, and the First and Eighth Army would encircle and destroy the trapped Axis forces. In the meantime, he intended to keep the central front quiet. Intelligence assessments seemed to support the idea that the decisive action would take place in northern Tunisia. The signals intelligence center at Bletchley Park was having a hard time decrypting the "Dodo" code used by Arnim's 5th Panzer Army but the Luftwaffe and Italian codes were proving to be more informative. On January 31, a message from the Luftwaffe commander in Tunisia laid out Arnim's plans for Operation *Kuckucksei* in some detail. Eisenhower's intelligence officer, Brigadier E.E. Mockler-Ferryman, concluded that the main German threat was an attack by 5th Panzer Army through the Fondouk Pass, which would then threaten the flank of British units in northern Tunisia.

On February 4, 1943 Bletchley Park sent Eisenhower's headquarters a decrypted copy of Rommel's plan for a more ambitious attack. Mockler-Ferryman put more credence in the earlier intercept since the message's Luftwaffe provenance suggested that this operation had already been

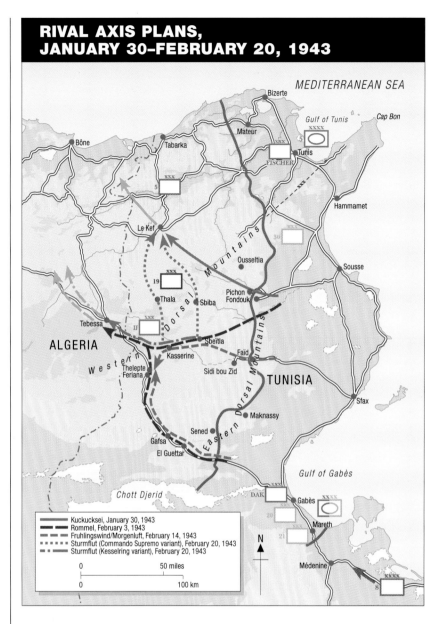

RIVAL AXIS PLANS, JANUARY 30–FEBRUARY 20, 1943

MEDITERRANEAN SEA

Bizerte

Gulf of Tunis

Cap Bon

Mateur

Bône

Tabarka

Tunis

FISCHER

Hammamet

Le Kef

Ousseltia

Sousse

Mountains

Pichon

Thala

Fondouk

Sbiba

Tebessa

Sbeïtla

ALGERIA

Kasserine

Faid

Thelepte

Sidi bou Zid

TUNISIA

Feriana

Maknassy

Sfax

Sened

Gafsa

El Guettar

Gulf of Gabès

Chott Djerid

DAK

Gabès

Mareth

N

Médenine

Kuckucksei, January 30, 1943
Rommel, February 3, 1943
Fruhlingswind/Morgenluft, February 14, 1943
Sturmflut (Commando Supremo variant), February 20, 1943
Sturmflut (Kesselring variant), February 20, 1943

| 0 | 50 miles |
| 0 | 100 km |

accepted, whereas Rommel's message was simply a proposed future operation. Later intercepts were misinterpreted to bolster this view. A February 8 Luftwaffe decrypt indicated that units would be moved to support the forthcoming 5th Panzer Army attack. On February 13, Enigma revealed that the headquarters of the 21st Panzer Division was deploying to its forward positions to begin the attack the following day, which Mockler-Ferryman interpreted to mean the Fondouk attack. Mockler-Ferryman conveyed this information to Anderson who alerted forward units to the threat, with a special emphasis on units around Fondouk. However, Anderson believed that the Germans might stage diversionary attacks, so other units including American units on the central front were also alerted for an attack on St Valentine's Day.

Allied intelligence had come to depend on the Enigma decrypts, especially following their stunning revelations during the El Alamein battles. But the Enigma decrypts, as good as they were, seldom revealed the whole picture. Intelligence assessments based in part on Enigma took on an air of infallibility even though they often contained the usual mixture of analysis and conjecture. Neither Anderson nor Eisenhower appreciated that Mockler-Ferryman's assessment was wrong and that tactical intelligence contradicted his interpretation of the incomplete Enigma information.

Due to this intelligence blunder, the Allied commanders continued to shuffle around the units in the II Corps area with little sense of urgency, instead of creating a cohesive defense. Anderson wanted to redeploy the French and Americans from their vulnerable and extended positions on the Eastern Dorsals and to concentrate their defenses on the eastern side of the Western Dorsals to keep them out of trouble. But Eisenhower's liaison officer Lucian Truscott pushed for a forward defense on the plains between the Dorsals. In the event, the issue was not finally settled prior to the German attack, and so US units remained scattered and unprepared.

For much of early February, Eisenhower was distracted by the need to attend the Casablanca conference with Roosevelt and Churchill. Eisenhower finally left the conference late on February 12 and arrived at the II Corps headquarters on February 13 for inspection. He was disturbed by what he found. Fredendall had established his command center in an inaccessible ravine and had used corps engineers to blast bombproof caves for the safety of the staff. The location of the command post was far to the rear, without easy access to the road network. Anderson visited Tebessa that day to consult with Fredendall and Eisenhower. He met with Fredendall's G-2 intelligence officer, Col. "Monk" Dickson, who argued that the tactical intelligence pointed to a German attack coming soon in the Gafsa area and possibly around Faïd as well, not Fondouk. Overly confident due to the Enigma decrypts, Anderson dismissed the American reports and warned Fredendall later that he had a "jumpy" staff officer. Anderson left abruptly later in the day when officers for his northern headquarters reported that a German attack in the north was imminent due to the latest decrypt. It is a sad irony that Dickson's warning was ignored in 1943, but nearly two years later when Dickson was G-2 for the US First Army, his assessment that the Germans would not strike in the Ardennes in December 1944 proved tragically wrong.

Eisenhower made a tour of forward positions later that day, and was disturbed at the complacency and lack of preparedness. Infantry units were deployed in the passes without minefields, merely with plans to start laying mines "tomorrow"—in contrast to the Germans who established minefields within hours of setting up their defenses. The situation with the 1st Armored Division was particularly unsettling and the division was badly scattered along 80 miles of front, contrary to Eisenhower's earlier instructions. Brig. Gen. Raymond McQuillin's CCA was 50 miles (80km) south around Sbeïtla. Brig. Gen. Paul Robinett's CCB had been operating in the north around Ousseltia since January 19 and was left in the area to help cover the northern sector in anticipation of the imminent launch of Operation *Kuckucksei*. Robinett, an old friend of Eisenhower, complained that his unit was being wasted as they had conducted deep penetrations behind the frontline and found no evidence of an impending German attack in this sector.

If the strategic posture of II Corps was poor, tactical deployments were little better. Fredendall ordered that the two task forces covering Kasserine Pass be deployed on two mountains, Djebel Lessouda and Ksaira on either side of the pass, but so far from each other that they could not provide mutual support. Fredendall later blamed Anderson for the details of the deployment, but in the event the precise deployment was irrelevant. Two reinforced infantry battalions had little hope of stopping two Panzer divisions, even if better deployed, since they could be outflanked or overrun. Given the enormous width of the front, a mobile reserve was needed to reinforce the scattered outposts and neither Anderson nor Fredendall had paid sufficient attention to Eisenhower's January 20 directive to concentrate more of the 1st Armored Division for this mission.

Eisenhower immediately issued a series of instructions to the various units to correct numerous deficiencies, but it was too late. By the time Eisenhower's group arrived back at II Corps headquarters that morning, the German assault had already begun.

THE CAMPAIGN

OPERATION *FRÜHLINGSWIND*: SIDI BOU ZID

Arnim's assault began in the early morning hours of February 14, 1943 and consisted of a two-pronged enveloping attack on Sidi bou Zid. The 10th Panzer Division debouched from Faïd Pass and swung around Djebel Lessouda to the northwest before descending on Sidi bou Zid, while the 21st Panzer Division emerged from the south through Maizila Pass. The CCA defenses on Djebel Lessouda consisted of the 2/168th Infantry of the 34th Division supported by a company of tanks and a platoon of tank destroyers and under the command of Patton's son-in-law, Lt. Col. John Waters. There was a similar force on the hill south of Sidi bou Zid, Djebel Ksaira, held by the 3/168th Infantry under Col. Thomas Drake deployed to block any advance from the south of Sidi bou Zid. The defensive scheme was for the infantry in the hill defenses to tie down any German forces coming out of Faïd Pass long enough to permit a counterattack by Lt. Col. Louis Hightower in Sid bou Zid with two companies of tanks and a dozen tank destroyers.

The 10th Panzer Division began moving around 0400 hours, completely enveloped in a sandstorm. Their lead Panzers overwhelmed a small American covering force as well as the hill's small armored contingent, Co. G, 1st Armored Regiment. Under the cover of the

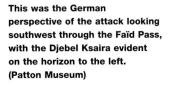

This was the German perspective of the attack looking southwest through the Faïd Pass, with the Djebel Ksaira evident on the horizon to the left. (Patton Museum)

sandstorm, one of the two battle groups swung around the western side of the hill to silence American artillery located there. By dawn, it was clear that a major attack was under way, but the storm made it impossible for the Americans on top of the hill to gauge its size. Around 0730 hours, the Luftwaffe staged a major air raid on Sidi bou Zid itself, devastating the town. By 0830 hours, the storm began to lift, and Col. Waters was finally able to see the advancing German force, which he estimated at 60 tanks, 20 other armored vehicles and numerous other vehicles. In the meantime, Hightower's armored force sallied out of Sidi bou Zid with two companies of M4 medium tanks, Cos. H and I, 1st Armored Regiment, and about a dozen tank destroyers of the 701st Tank Destroyer Battalion. As Hightower's force closed on the German attack, he quickly realized he was badly outnumbered and radioed back to the commander of CCA, Col. McQuillin, that the best he could do would be to delay them. Hightower's tanks were already being hit by a battery of 88mm guns deployed at the base of Djebel Lessouda and by long-range 88mm fire from Tiger tanks. He attempted to fight a withdrawing action back to Sidi bou Zid, but was fully engaged by 1030 hours; his outnumbered force was gradually shot to pieces. Waters and the 2/168th Infantry were completely isolated on the upper side of Djebel Lessouda, little able to influence the battle, and for the time being were ignored by the advancing 10th Panzer Division.

While the situation around Djebel Lessouda developed, the attack by 21st Panzer Division began to emerge from the southern approaches of Sidi bou Zid, but more slowly as the sandstorm had been more intense and longer lasting in this sector. Kampfgruppe Schütte, built around Panzergrenadier Regiment 104 and supported by a detachment of tanks, moved to the west of the 3/168th Infantry defenses on Djebel Ksaira around noon, while Kampfgruppe Stenkhoff with the bulk of

The attack on Djebel Lessouda was supported by Tiger heavy tanks of s.Pz.Abt. 501. This one was captured later in the campaign and shipped back to the US; it is seen here on display in Washington, DC in February 1944. (MHI)

A US infantry 37mm anti-tank gun squad sets up its weapon on February 14, 1943, the day of the German attack. Djebel Lessouda, where one of the US infantry battalions was trapped, can be seen in the background. (MHI)

A platoon of M4A1 medium tanks of Hightower's 3/1st Armored, blasted by the 10th Panzer Division on the approaches to Djebel Lessouda. The town of Sidi bou Zid and Djebel Ksaira are evident in the background. (Patton Museum)

A surviving M4A1 medium tank from Co.G, 3/1st Armored retrieving a disabled M3 halftrack after the ill-fated attempt to stop the encirclement of 3/168th Infantry atop Djebel Lessouda, which can be seen in the background. (NARA)

Panzer Regiment 5, moved behind Sidi bou Zid from the southwest around 1400 hours after having taken the longer route around Djebel el Kebar.

By noon, German tanks were approaching McQuillin's command post in Sidi bou Zid from multiple directions and the town was under direct tank fire. Hightower had already lost more than half of his tanks in a valiant but futile effort to halt the 10th Panzer Division. Hightower's tank knocked out four German tanks before finally being hit and burned; he and his crew walked from the battle back towards Sbeïtla. Only seven tanks of Hightower's original force of 44 survived the day. McQuillin first evacuated most of the CCA troops except for his immediate staff, and withdrew to a temporary command post west of the town shortly after noon. Drake's force on Djebel Ksaira still had some hope of escaping, but permission was denied by Fredendall at 1410 hours. Lacking any further communication from headquarters, Drake moved part of his force to the neighboring and more defensible Garet Hadid on the opposite side of the pass. With the situation around Sidi bou Zid collapsing, McQuillin's executive officer, Col. Peter Hains, drove to the 1st Armored Division headquarters near Sbeïtla and begged

Gen. Ward to permit Waters and Drake to withdraw from their hopeless positions. Ward explained that Fredendall had refused permission, and that a counterattack was being planned. Fredendall's rigid command style and his remote command post doomed the two isolated battalions.

The spearheads of the 10th and 21st Panzer Divisions made contact to the west of Sidi bou Zid shortly before nightfall and consolidated their positions around the town. So far, Operation *Frühlingswind* had gone as planned and German casualties were light. In the fields around Sidi bou Zid were 44 American tanks, 59 half-tracks, 26 artillery pieces and 22 trucks either knocked out or abandoned. Gen. Heinz Ziegler, Arnim's deputy, was the tactical commander of the operation and he decided to remain near Sidi bou Zid that night in anticipation of an American counterattack. Ziegler's extreme caution infuriated Rommel, who telephoned Arnim and urged him to press Ziegler forward at night towards Sbeïtla to exploit the success. Arnim shared Ziegler's cautious approach and wanted to preserve his forces for later operations towards Pichon and the north as in his original *Kuckucksei* plan.

The response from senior Allied commanders was wary but not overly alarmed. Anderson was convinced that the Sidi bou Zid attack was merely a diversion to mask the expected attack towards Fondouk. He pointed to the absence of the 10th Panzer Division in attack as evidence, which was of course erroneous. Ward wanted all of Robinett's CCB diverted from the Fondouk area to Sbeïtla, but in light of Anderson's assessment, he authorized the transfer of only a single tank battalion. Lt. Col. James Alger's 2/1st Armored Regiment arrived around Sbeïtla the evening of February 14. German activity around Gafsa convinced Fredendall that another blow was about to take place, and he received permission to begin withdrawing French and US troops.

Ward believed that McQuillin had exaggerated German strength around Sidi bou Zid, since Allied intelligence was still claiming that only one Panzer division was involved. He thus estimated the German composition around Sidi bou Zid to be about 40 tanks around Djebel Lessouda and 20 near Djebel Ksaira. The counterattack planned for the next day would be led by Col. Robert Stack consisting of Alger's medium tank battalion in the lead, supported by a company of M3 75mm tank destroyers from the 701st Tank Destroyer Battalion on the flanks, and followed by two batteries of self-propelled artillery and the 3/6th Armored Infantry in halftracks. In hindsight, it is remarkable that such a meager and inexperienced force was expected to accomplish anything, without any preparatory reconnaissance. At a minimum, the Germans in Sidi bou Zid

Alger's 2/1st Armored Regiment was slaughtered in the Oued Rouana wadi outside Sidi bou Zid on February 15 by the combined firepower of two Panzer divisions. The vehicles shown here are an M4A1 to the left and an M4 medium tank to the right from Company F. (NARA)

consisted of at least a Panzer division, presumably dug in to repulse a counterattack from prepared defensive positions. In reality, a single battalion of tanks and a battalion of mechanized infantry were being sent to confront two combat-hardened Panzer divisions. The results were tragically predictable.

Stack's counterattack began at 1240 hours on February 15 in textbook fashion, with Alger's medium tanks in a broad V formation. A Luftwaffe observation plane spotted the preparations and warned Ziegler's force of their location and direction. The Germans had had plenty of time to prepare the defenses since the night before, and had set up anti-tank guns and a battery of four 88mm Flak guns in olive groves to cover the obvious approach route in the open country to the northwest of Sidi bou Zid. Elements of Panzer Regiment 5 were sent out to the west with the aim of coming upon the American flank from the south, while the 21st Panzer Division deployed a similar force from the north. The Germans allowed the first wave of tanks to pass through the concealed anti-tank gun screen. As the anti-tank guns began to open fire, the American tank companies tried to maneuver for defense, but the terrain was too open to provide much cover. As evidence of the German tanks on either flank became apparent, one tank company attempted to deal with the northern group from 21st Panzer Division, while another attempted to deal with the force from the 10th Panzer Division to the south. Alger's tank battalion was cut off from the accompanying infantry and by late afternoon, it was clear they would never make it anywhere near their objective of Djebel Ksaira and the trapped 3/168th Infantry. Some four tanks towards the rear of the battalion managed to retreat with the half-track infantry around 1740 hours, but the remaining 40 tanks of Alger's battalion clustered in Oued Rouana wadi, where they were gradually shot to bits by the encircling German tanks and anti-tank guns in a mechanized version of "Custer's Last Stand."

There was considerable confusion the night of February 15 as to what had happened. Ward reported: "Lot of burning tanks east of Sidi bou Zid. Don't know who they belong to yet. We might have walloped them

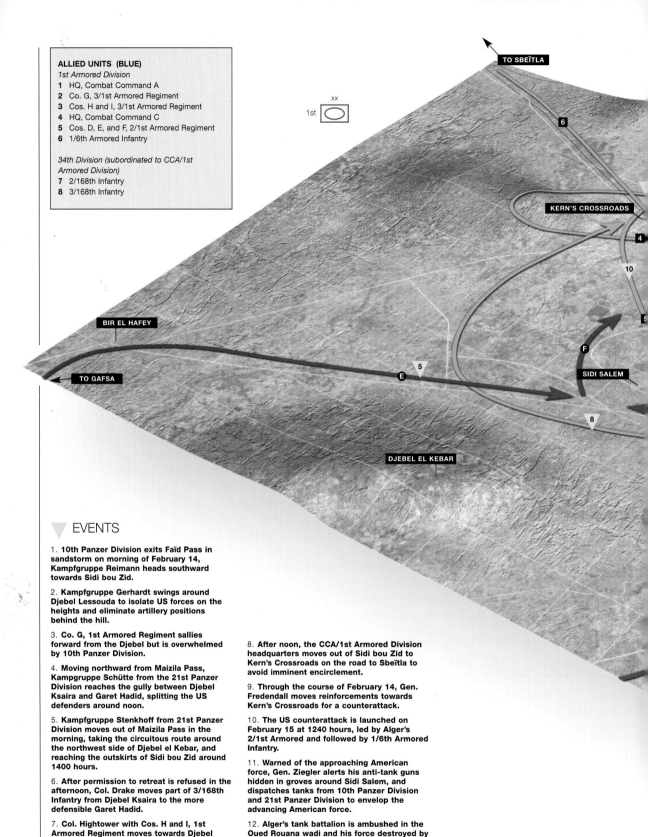

ALLIED UNITS (BLUE)
1st Armored Division
1 HQ, Combat Command A
2 Co. G, 3/1st Armored Regiment
3 Cos. H and I, 3/1st Armored Regiment
4 HQ, Combat Command C
5 Cos. D, E, and F, 2/1st Armored Regiment
6 1/6th Armored Infantry

34th Division (subordinated to CCA/1st Armored Division)
7 2/168th Infantry
8 3/168th Infantry

XX
1st

TO SBEÏTLA

6

KERN'S CROSSROADS

4

10

BIR EL HAFEY

TO GAFSA

5

E

F

SIDI SALEM

8

DJEBEL EL KEBAR

▼ EVENTS

1. **10th Panzer Division exits Faïd Pass in sandstorm on morning of February 14, Kampfgruppe Reimann heads southward towards Sidi bou Zid.**

2. **Kampfgruppe Gerhardt swings around Djebel Lessouda to isolate US forces on the heights and eliminate artillery positions behind the hill.**

3. **Co. G, 1st Armored Regiment sallies forward from the Djebel but is overwhelmed by 10th Panzer Division.**

4. **Moving northward from Maizila Pass, Kampfgruppe Schütte from the 21st Panzer Division reaches the gully between Djebel Ksaira and Garet Hadid, splitting the US defenders around noon.**

5. **Kampfgruppe Stenkhoff from 21st Panzer Division moves out of Maizila Pass in the morning, taking the circuitous route around the northwest side of Djebel el Kebar, and reaching the outskirts of Sidi bou Zid around 1400 hours.**

6. **After permission to retreat is refused in the afternoon, Col. Drake moves part of 3/168th Infantry from Djebel Ksaira to the more defensible Garet Hadid.**

7. **Col. Hightower with Cos. H and I, 1st Armored Regiment moves towards Djebel Lessouda mid-morning, and fights a costly delaying action against lead elements of the 10th Panzer Division before being overwhelmed.**

8. **After noon, the CCA/1st Armored Division headquarters moves out of Sidi bou Zid to Kern's Crossroads on the road to Sbeïtla to avoid imminent encirclement.**

9. **Through the course of February 14, Gen. Fredendall moves reinforcements towards Kern's Crossroads for a counterattack.**

10. **The US counterattack is launched on February 15 at 1240 hours, led by Alger's 2/1st Armored and followed by 1/6th Armored Infantry.**

11. **Warned of the approaching American force, Gen. Ziegler alerts his anti-tank guns hidden in groves around Sidi Salem, and dispatches tanks from 10th Panzer Division and 21st Panzer Division to envelop the advancing American force.**

12. **Alger's tank battalion is ambushed in the Oued Rouana wadi and his force destroyed by hidden anti-tank guns and attacking Panzers on either side in the late afternoon. The 1/6th Armored Infantry manages to retreat back to Kern's Crossroads after nightfall.**

SIDI BOU ZID, FEBRUARY 14–15, 1943

US 1st Armored Division is overwhelmed at Faïd Pass.

Note: the gridlines shown lie at intervals of 2 miles.

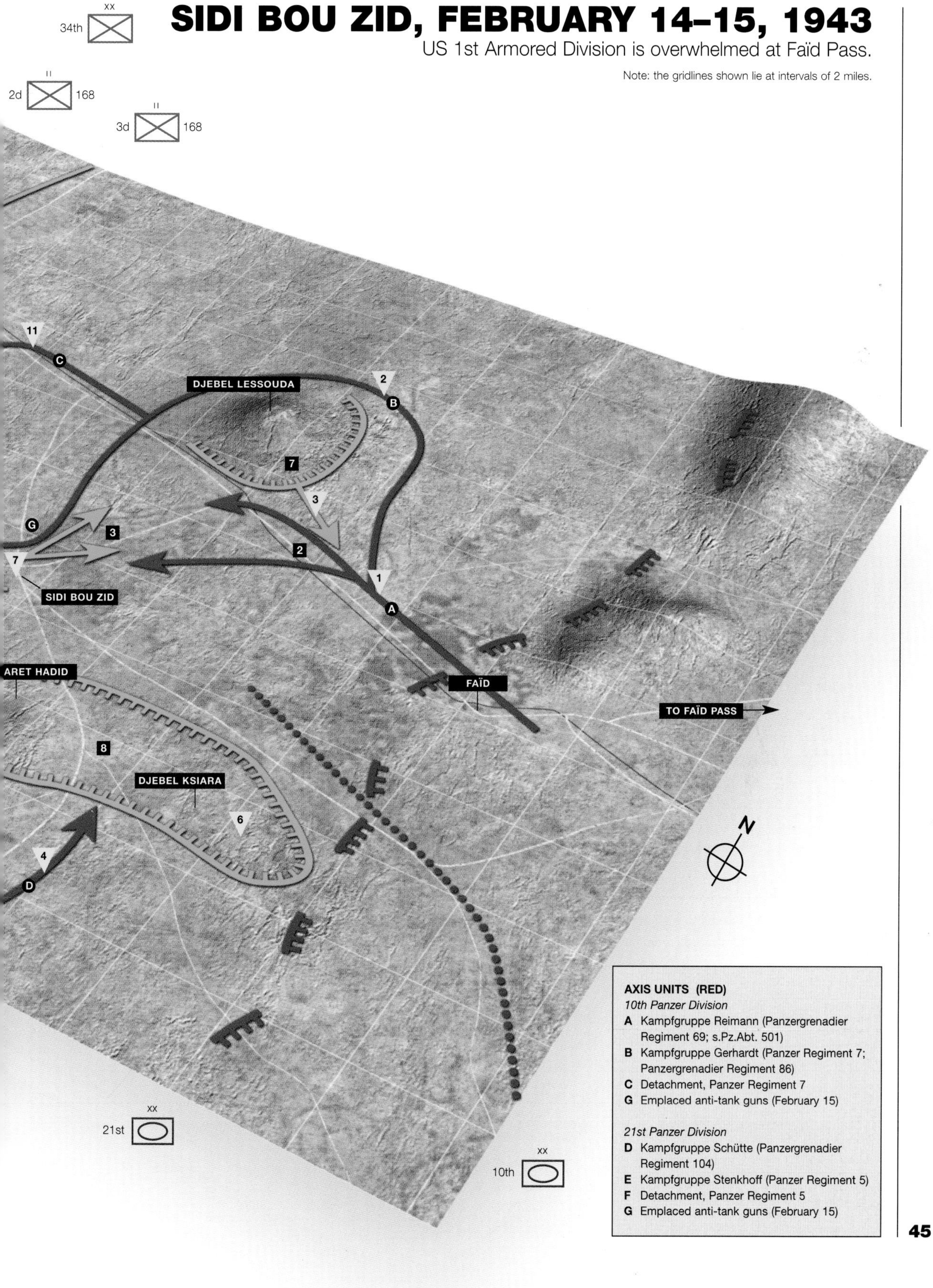

34th

2d 168

3d 168

11

C

DJEBEL LESSOUDA

2

B

7

3

G

3

2

7

1

SIDI BOU ZID

A

ARET HADID

FAÏD

TO FAÏD PASS

8

DJEBEL KSIARA

6

4

D

N

21st

10th

AXIS UNITS (RED)

10th Panzer Division

A Kampfgruppe Reimann (Panzergrenadier
   Regiment 69; s.Pz.Abt. 501)
B Kampfgruppe Gerhardt (Panzer Regiment 7;
   Panzergrenadier Regiment 86)
C Detachment, Panzer Regiment 7
G Emplaced anti-tank guns (February 15)

21st Panzer Division

D Kampfgruppe Schütte (Panzergrenadier
   Regiment 104)
E Kampfgruppe Stenkhoff (Panzer Regiment 5)
F Detachment, Panzer Regiment 5
G Emplaced anti-tank guns (February 15)

One of the few survivors of the destruction of 2/1st Armored was this M4A1 of Company E seen here after the Kasserine fighting.

or they might have walloped us." But it was apparent that the attack had failed to relieve the two trapped battalions on the hills on either side of Kasserine Pass. Two P-39 fighters were ordered to fly over the djebels and drop messages to the surrounded US battalions to escape. In two days of fighting, CCA had lost two tank and two infantry battalions without causing any appreciable loss to the Germans.

In spite of the magnitude of the victory, Ziegler did not exploit his success. He sent reconnaissance patrols towards Sbeïtla to determine whether the Americans might try another counterattack. On hearing this, Rommel was enraged at the lost opportunity, but Kesselring was at the Führer headquarters in East Prussia that day and could not intervene. Arnim was more concerned about wasting fuel, which he wished to conserve for later operations around Fondouk, and his units had already accomplished their intended mission of crushing CCA.

Kesselring didn't learn of Arnim's success until February 16, and he relayed instructions to Arnim through the Comando Supremo to take Sbeïtla. Ziegler continued to dither and reinforced his earlier reconnaissance mission with a small detachment of tanks near the road junction the Americans called "Kern's Crossroads." This gave the Allies more time to prepare their defenses. Anderson finally began to recognize that his intelligence assessments were completely wrong, and he ordered Koeltz to move his French corps back to the Western Dorsals, including the elements of the US 34th Infantry Division under his command. Fredendall asked Anderson to free up British troops to hold the key pass at Sbiba in the Western Dorsals, which he agreed to do. The British 26th Armoured Brigade and two battalions of infantry were positioned south and east of Sbiba. Ward was allowed to withdraw the rest of Robinett's CCB to Sbeïtla, finally consolidating most of the division in one area after months of dispersion. On the night of February 16, US forces pulled back from their easternmost position at Kern's Crossroads, buoyed by a minor success when a few US tanks ambushed the Panzers of Ziegler's forward detachment.

When a second American counterattack failed to materialize on February 16, Ziegler belatedly decided to press on to Sbeïtla the next day, a decision reinforced by a stern Comando Supremo instruction. The Allied withdrawal from Gafsa had allowed Rommel's Operation *Morgenluft* to begin, and Gen. Kurt Liebenstein had already occupied the town with troops of the Afrika Korps after the Allied troops had withdrawn. Rommel instructed Liebenstein to continue his unopposed advance up the road towards Feriana to support Arnim's attack.

CONFUSION AT SBEÏTLA

During the evening of February 16, the survivors of CCA had set up defenses in the olive groves north of Sbeïtla while Robinett's newly arrived and more experienced CCB held the southern perimeter. Advance elements of Ziegler's command probed the outer defenses with sporadic machine gun and artillery fire. When the CCA headquarters in the olive grove came under machine gun fire, McQuillin decided to shift his staff to the west side of Sbeïtla and out of harm's way, little appreciating the consequences this would have for neighboring units. After having seen two of their battalions left to their fate on Djebel Lessouda and Ksaira and both hasty tank counterattacks pulverized, the remaining units of CCA were demoralized. Amidst the sounds of explosions as engineers demolished an ammunition dump and several structures, some units near the withdrawing headquarters assumed a retreat was under way, and began retreating out of Sbeïtla without orders. CCA disintegrated. Wild rumors spread and the sight of retreating, panicked troops encouraged other jumpy troops to follow. The roads out of Sbeïtla were a traffic jam of fleeing troops and vehicles.

Fortunately, the battle-hardened troops of Robinett's CCB, and a few CCA units held their ground and kept the German units at bay for the remainder of the night. At dawn, officers set up roadblocks and began collecting the numerous deserters on the outskirts of the town. Ziegler's

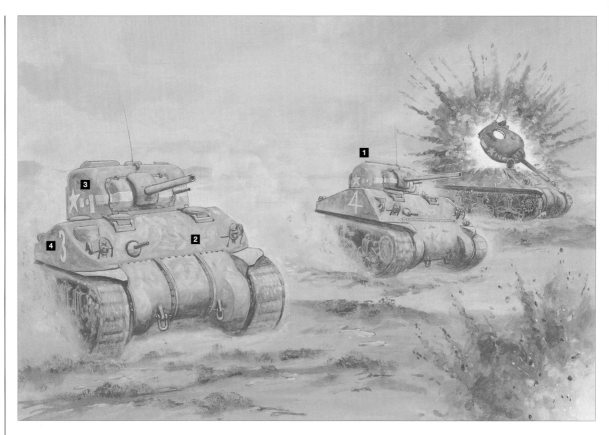

THE CHARGE OF 2/1ST ARMORED AT SIDI BOU ZID, FEBRUARY 15, 1943 (pp 48–49)

The tank charge by the 2d Battalion, 1st Armored Regiment of the 1st Armored Division at Sidi bou Zid on February 15, 1943 was a case study in military failure. Two inexperienced battalions were sent across open desert against two experienced German Panzer divisions already well emplaced in defensive positions, with predictable consequences. There were no tactics worthy of the term: Alger's battalion simply headed forward in a cavalry charge intending to collide with the Germans somewhere near Sidi bou Zid. The 2/1st Armored had never seen combat, and like the rest of 1st Armored Division, had not participated in tank-vs.-tank tactical training at the Desert Training Center in the Mojave Desert due to the rush to deploy it into the combat theater. Instead of following the German tactics of slow movement in the desert to minimize dust, the battalion advanced towards the German positions at moderate speed. As a result, the American tanks were clearly visible to the German anti-tank gunners, while at the same time the cloud of dust kicked up by neighboring tanks blinded the US tankers from seeing the threats around them. The tanks attacked in a rough "V" formation in alphabetical order: Co. D on the left, Co. E in the center, and Co. F on the right. The outlying tank companies did spot the German outflanking maneuver. However, by the time they recognized the threat, the lead tanks had already moved within range

of the camouflaged German anti-tank gun emplacements in the olive groves around them, and came under fire. The Germans were able to move two tank battalions on either side of Alger's battalion and mercilessly blast his trapped tanks from three sides. Alger's unit claimed to have knocked out 19 German tanks. Only four of his tanks survived, those near the rear of the advancing column that retreated back to Kern's Crossroads with the 1/6th Armored Infantry when Alger's battalion was trapped. The illustration on the previous pages depicts the charge as it is taken under fire by the German anti-tank guns. The 2/1st Armored was equipped with M4 (1) and M4A1 (2) medium tanks. These were essentially identical except that the M4 had a welded upper hull while the M4A1 featured a cast upper hull. The M4 was an excellent tank for its day, with a good combination of armor, firepower and mobility. It was certainly the equal of the better German tanks such as the PzKpfw IV Ausf. F, and the M4 was better than other common German types such as the PzKpfw III. The 10th Panzer Division had a Tiger battalion at Sidi bou Zid, but it did not take part in the fighting on February 15. The Tigers had participated in the annihilation of Hightower's battalion on February 14, claiming the destruction of 20 Sherman tanks that day. The M4 was certainly no equal to the Tiger, but there were very few Tigers in action in Tunisia. The unit company markings are shown on the turrets of the M4 tanks (3), with the individual tank numbers on the side (4).

forces were not able to profit from the panic in Sbeïtla, but confused reports of the situation in Sbeïtla convinced Fredendall that the town was about to fall. Anderson instructed him to hold the town until the evening of February 17, but Fredendall warned that it could collapse at any moment. As a result, Anderson authorized a withdrawal at 1100 hours. Gen. Ward was instructed to retire through Kasserine Pass towards Thala, and Col. Anderson Moore was ordered to deploy his 19th Engineer Regiment across the Hatab riverbed east of Kasserine on the road from Sbeïtla to cover the 1st Armored Division during their withdrawal.

Ziegler's attack into Sbeïtla was postponed yet again by unexpected developments in his rear near Faïd Pass. The two American infantry battalions in the hills west of the pass had been bypassed but not mopped up due to the difficulties presented by the hilly terrain. A German infantry battalion attempted to take Djebel Ksaira on February 15, but were unable to do so due to stiff resistance. After Drake had been instructed by the air-delivered message that night to fight his way out, his battalion brazenly began marching in daylight the eight miles to Sbeïtla through scattered and thinly held German rear area positions. Drake's men destroyed a scout car, and the Germans finally realized that the columns marching across the barren plains west of Faïd were the missing American troops, not German troops. Ziegler postponed the attack on Sbeïtla to send units back to the pass to clean up other escaping American infantry units.

The German probes into Sbeïtla began in the afternoon of February 17. Little realizing the predicament of CCA's weak defenses, the main German push took place south of town against the more solid defenses of Robinett's CCB. Col. Henry Gardiner's 2/13th Armored, although at less than half strength on account of continual combat since December, met the initial German Panzer attack with a carefully planned ambush. Gardiner's tanks claimed 15 Panzers; the Germans admitted five. While CCB was holding off the attack, CCA suffered another wave of panic and disintegration, and many of its units withdrew even without contact with the Germans. Robinett's CCB remained in position until late afternoon, and began withdrawing in good order shortly before 1700 hours. CCB reached Kasserine Pass shortly after nightfall and took up positions on the road towards Thala. One of the casualties during the Sbeïtla fighting

An SdKfz 233 heavy armored car abandoned in Sbeïtla after the fighting there. This version of the SdKfz 231 family was used to provide fire support in German reconnaissance battalions, and was armed with a short 75mm howitzer. (NARA)

was Col. Henry Gardiner's command tank, but he managed to walk back to American lines near Kasserine and rejoin his unit a day later.

OPERATION *MORGENLUFT*

Rommel's *Morgenluft* operation began after Arnim's, but faced little opposition. Gafsa was occupied after it had been abandoned by Allied units, and Kampfgruppe DAK under Gen. Liebenstein continued up the road to Feriana on February 17. When Liebenstein was wounded by a mine, the battlegroup was taken over by Gen. Karl Bülowius, the former Afrika Korps artillery commander. The big prize of the day was the airfield at Thelepte. Although abandoned by the Allies the previous day, the battlegroup managed to salvage nearly 50 tons of fuel and lubricants from the partially destroyed stores at the base, along with other supplies. Rommel was delighted by the easy advance of his forces, but in reality the outcome had been determined by the advance of Arnim's forces against Kasserine Pass. On the night of February 17, the Comando Supremo sent instructions that Kampfgruppe DAK would stick to the original plan and stop at the line of Gafsa–Metlaoui–Tozeur. Several units were withdrawn back towards Gafsa for return to the Mareth Line, but Rommel managed to send some reconnaissance units towards Kasserine Pass. An Afrika Korps detachment rolled into Kasserine, capturing 60 French troops, and meeting a reconnaissance group from the 21st Panzer Division.

In spite of the dismal state of the US 1st Armored Division in the wake of the previous days' fighting, Arnim had no intentions to pursue. On the evening of February 17 he decided to break up the attack force, sending the 10th Panzer Division north towards the Fondouk and Pinchon passes, and leaving the 21st Panzer Division at Sbeïtla. In a phone conversation on the evening of February 17 with Rommel, he blamed his precarious supply of fuel and supplies. In exasperation over a discarded opportunity, Rommel sent a message to Kesselring on February 18 asking that Arnim's battlegroup be turned over to his command to launch an attack through Kasserine Pass to the main Allied supply center at Tebessa, and then on to the coast at Bone. Kesselring was more enthusiastic about such an operation than Arnim, but needed the formalities of a meeting with the Comando Supremo and Mussolini himself before he could confirm such a major shift in force deployments. The approval for Rommel's plan did not arrive in Tunisia until midnight, February 18–19, after yet another day had been wasted.

The Comando Supremo plan shifted both the 10th and 21st Panzer Divisions to Rommel's command. The revised Operation *Sturmflut* (Stormflood) had the immediate objective to strike northwestward through Kasserine Pass to Le Kef, a shallow envelopment behind the positions of the British First Army. Arnim was ordered to support Rommel's attack by tying down Anderson's forces in northern Tunisia, and by staging a paratroop drop near Le Kef to destroy key bridges and prevent Allied forces from retreating. Both Kesselring and Rommel had mixed feelings about *Sturmflut*, believing that such a shallow envelopment was mistaken instead of the more lucrative objective of Tebessa and Rommel's proposed deep envelopment of the First Army. In spite of his disappointment, at least he had a commitment to continue the offensive.

For Operation *Sturmflut*, Group Rommel included the 10th and 21st Panzer Division, Kampfgruppe DAK and the Italian Centauro armored division. Rommel's former command, the German–Italian Panzer Army at the Mareth Line, was finally turned over to Gen. Messe, being renamed the 1st Italian Army.

The bickering and lack of consensus within the Axis high command led to a dispersion in forces after the fall of Sbeïtla. Rather than wait to re-concentrate his units, Rommel decided to strike as quickly as possible to take advantage of the confusion in the Allied ranks, and also to prevent the Comando Supremo from changing their minds. His plan was to push the 21st Panzer Division through the Sbiba Gap towards the main objective of Le Kef. Kampfgruppe DAK would push through the Kasserine Pass while the Centauro Division would advance through the Dernaia Pass. Once the 10th Panzer Division had returned from the Pinchon area, it would reinforce whichever of the two main thrusts were showing the best results.

Kesselring visited Tunisia on February 19 to ensure that Arnim supported Rommel's attack. To his surprise, Arnim offered a counter-proposal: a broader offensive in Tunisia with the 10th Panzer Division striking from its existing positions near Pinchon. But Kesselring was more sympathetic to Rommel's vision of an offensive oriented towards Tebessa, and more confident that he would carry out such a bold plan. Arnim had not conducted the *Frühlingswind* operation with any particular enthusiasm, even after he had succeeded in routing the American forces around Sidi bou Zid. Although Kesselring had hoped that Rommel would take matters in his own hands and place the emphasis of his attack towards Tebessa, he did not explicitly say so in his instructions and Rommel was left with the understanding that the Comando Supremo wanted the main thrust directed towards Sbiba and then to Le Kef. Regardless of the focus of the attack, Rommel wanted Kasserine Pass seized to prevent the Allies from sending forces from the Tebessa area against his exposed left flank.

The Allied defenses in the Western Dorsals were uneven, with the strongest concentrations to the north near Sbiba. The US 34th Division had arrived to reinforce the French 19th Corps and Anderson had shifted the 6th Armoured Division into the area, with the 26th Armoured Brigade defending the key road junction at Thala. Access to the Allied supply center at Tebessa was through several possible routes, including the mountain passes at Elma Labiod, Bou Chebko and Kasserine, and the city was shielded by the remnants of the French Constantine Division along with the CCB/1st Armored Division near Bou Chebko, and the CCA still in transit to the area. As a result, the route to Sbiba and the southern passes towards Tebessa were the best guarded, while Kasserine Pass was tenuously held by a scratch force.

OPERATION *STURMFLUT*: THE BATTLE FOR KASSERINE PASS

Kasserine Pass was initially defended by Col. Anderson Moore's 19th Engineer Regiment. Although the engineers had some nominal training as infantry, they were primarily a construction unit with no experienced infantry officers. A defensive line was created across the narrowest section of the pass, approximately 800 yards in width. This also covered the road through the pass before it split in two, the northern spur going to Thala and the other spur going to Tebessa. Aside from the mountains, the other distinguishing geographic feature of the position was the Hatab River, in full flood, which bisected the pass. A large number of mines had been delivered to the engineers, but they had arrived so late that some of the minefields were very hasty, with mines simply laid on the ground or lightly covered with soil with little attempt at concealment. Prior to the German attack, the engineers were reinforced by the 1/26th Infantry, which took over defense of the hilly northeast shoulder on Djebel Semmama. There were three companies of engineers to the south of the river, and one company to the north

A view of the rugged terrain around Kasserine Pass looking from the west towards the narrowest part of the pass where the roads to Thala (to the left) and Tebessa (to the right) diverge. The Hatab riverbed is clearly evident here, but was in full flood at the time of the battle. (Patton Museum)

along with the infantry battalion in the hills. These units were supported by eight M4 tanks of Co. I, 13th Armored and the M3 75mm GMCs of the 894th Tank Destroyer Battalion in the center of the valley. Fire support came from two 105mm howitzer batteries of the 33d Field Artillery Battalion and a French horse-drawn 75mm battery. Fredendall was concerned about the lack of infantry experience of the engineers, so hours before the German attack he directed Col. Alexander Stark of the 26th Infantry to take control of the force.

Rommel decided to launch the attack with Kampfgruppe DAK commanded by Gen. Karl Bülowius since the 10th Panzer Division was still en route. He hoped that American defenses were so disorganized that it might be possible to seize them on the run. Reconnaissance Battalion 33 began the attack around 0630 hours on February 19, attempting to move through the pass and seize the Chebko Pass outlets further down the valley. They soon discovered that the defenses were already well in place and the concentration of tanks, infantry and tank destroyers in the center of the pass opened fire, forcing the battalion to move to the cover of the foothills of Djebel Chambi on the southwest side of the pass. After this rebuff, Bülowius ordered Panzergrenadier Regiment Afrika forward in its 40 trucks, and two battalions started an attack on the opposite side of the pass against the 1/26th Infantry around 0930 hours. The defenses were in the hills at the base of Djebel Semmama, and the German infantry had a difficult time seizing the key hilltops. As a result, Bülowius was forced to commit his main tank support, Panzer Battalion Stotten, around noon. Kampfgruppe DAK was unable to break through the pass on the first day of the attack, and at nightfall fighting continued on both sides of the pass, with the Germans trying to infiltrate past the American defenses through the mountainous terrain.

Brigadier Charles Dunphie, commanding the British 26th Armoured Brigade in Thala, visited Stark during the day and was alarmed at the tenuous defenses and the evidence of German infiltration in the hills above the pass. After informing Anderson's headquarters of his concerns, a First Army staff officer visited Stark that night but found the situation to be quiet. Nevertheless, Anderson gave Dunphie permission to place a blocking force along the road to Thala in case the defense

55

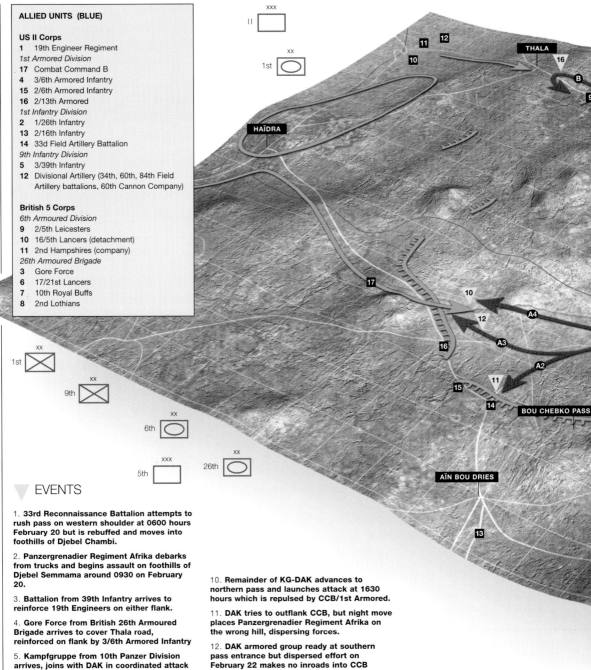

ALLIED UNITS (BLUE)

US II Corps
1   19th Engineer Regiment
1st Armored Division
17 Combat Command B
4   3/6th Armored Infantry
15 2/6th Armored Infantry
16 2/13th Armored
1st Infantry Division
2   1/26th Infantry
13 2/16th Infantry
14 33d Field Artillery Battalion
9th Infantry Division
5   3/39th Infantry
12 Divisional Artillery (34th, 60th, 84th Field
    Artillery battalions, 60th Cannon Company)

British 5 Corps
6th Armoured Division
9   2/5th Leicesters
10 16/5th Lancers (detachment)
11 2nd Hampshires (company)
26th Armoured Brigade
3   Gore Force
6   17/21st Lancers
7   10th Royal Buffs
8   2nd Lothians

▼ EVENTS

1. **33rd Reconnaissance Battalion attempts to rush pass on western shoulder at 0600 hours February 20 but is rebuffed and moves into foothills of Djebel Chambi.**

2. **Panzergrenadier Regiment Afrika debarks from trucks and begins assault on foothills of Djebel Semmama around 0930 on February 20.**

3. **Battalion from 39th Infantry arrives to reinforce 19th Engineers on either flank.**

4. **Gore Force from British 26th Armoured Brigade arrives to cover Thala road, reinforced on flank by 3/6th Armored Infantry**

5. **Kampfgruppe from 10th Panzer Division arrives, joins with DAK in coordinated attack around 1630 hours on February 20.**

6. **US tanks and tank destroyers along road overwhelmed, 19th Engineer defenses crumble by early evening of February 20.**

7. **An armored battalion of Centauro Division serves as DAK vanguard and races down road, reaching the exits of Bou Chebko Pass around nightfall.**

8. **10th Panzer Division overwhelms Gore Force by evening of February 20; 3/6 Armored Infantry and 1/16th Infantry encircled in hills over the pass.**

9. **Centauro vanguard encounters a CCB outpost about 0500 hours on February 21, which withdraws around dawn.**

10. **Remainder of KG-DAK advances to northern pass and launches attack at 1630 hours which is repulsed by CCB/1st Armored.**

11. **DAK tries to outflank CCB, but night move places Panzergrenadier Regiment Afrika on the wrong hill, dispersing forces.**

12. **DAK armored group ready at southern pass entrance but dispersed effort on February 22 makes no inroads into CCB defense. Withdrawal begins at 1415 hours.**

13. **10th Panzer Division at outpost position of 26 Armoured Brigade by morning of 21 February.**

14. **Next defensive line of 26th Armoured Brigade overwhelmed around 1600 hours.**

15. **Germans enter final 26th Armoured Brigade defensive positions using captured Valentine tank, wild mêlée begins after dark.**

16. **Attempt to break into Thala at 0700 hours, February 22 rebuffed by stiff British resistance and heavy artillery barrage by newly arrived divisional artillery of US 9th Infantry Division. German retreat begins in afternoon.**

KASSERINE PASS, FEBRUARY 20–22, 1943

Rommel's attack is checked at Kasserine Pass.

Note: the gridlines are at intervals of 2 miles.

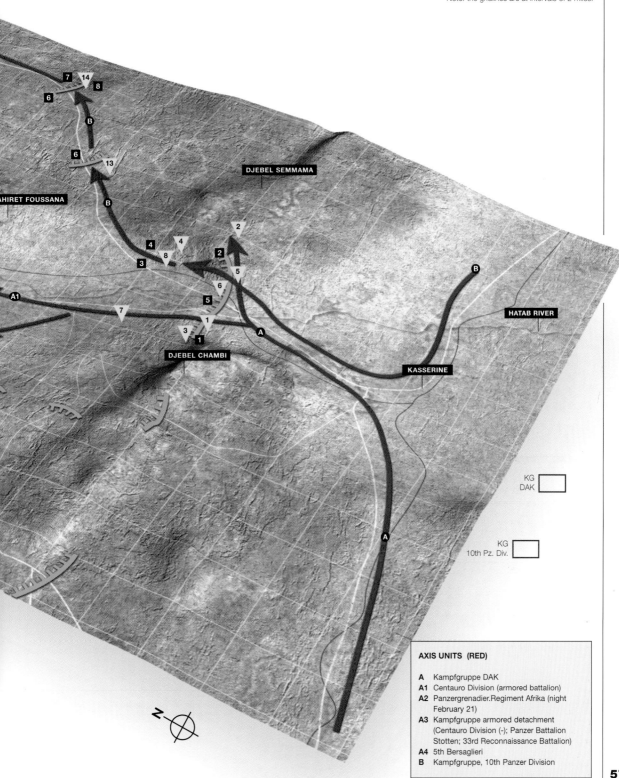

DJEBEL SEMMAMA

AHIRET FOUSSANA

HATAB RIVER

KASSERINE

DJEBEL CHAMBI

KG
DAK

KG
10th Pz. Div.

AXIS UNITS (RED)

A   Kampfgruppe DAK
A1 Centauro Division (armored battalion)
A2 Panzergrenadier.Regiment Afrika (night February 21)
A3 Kampfgruppe armored detachment (Centauro Division (-); Panzer Battalion Stotten; 33rd Reconnaissance Battalion)
A4 5th Bersaglieri
B   Kampfgruppe, 10th Panzer Division

57

crumpled. Gore Force under Lt. Col. A. Gore of the 10th Battalion, Royal Buffs consisted of seven Valentine and four Crusader tanks of C Squadron, 2nd Lothians, a company of motorized infantry and a battery of artillery. Lt. Col. W. Wells' 3/6th Armored Infantry, 1st Armored Division arrived late on February 19, and Stark sent them into the hills to cover Gore Force. Other reinforcements had trickled in to Stark through the day, including an infantry battalion from the 39th Infantry, 9th Division, and another tank destroyer battalion. Two of the infantry companies were deployed on the extreme flanks of the engineer companies in the line across the western side of the pass.

A US engineer prepares a minefield during the Tunisian fighting. (NARA)

After dark, the German infantry continued its attempts to infiltrate past US positions, and managed to take a few hilltops. A night attack by the 1/26th Infantry recaptured Hill 700 but one of its companies was cut off and its headquarters surrounded by infiltrating German infantry. Engineer defenses on the north side of the Hatab River had crumbled, though the lines to the south of the river covering the Tebessa road continued to hold. The 894th Tank Destroyer Battalion had lost half of its self-propelled guns during the day's fighting, and the two US artillery batteries were pulling back without orders, leaving only the French 75mm battery. Fredendall alerted Robinett's CCB to be ready to move to block the pass behind the engineers.

The morning of February 20 was cold and rainy, and the pass slippery with mud. Rommel appeared in Kasserine and was very displeased when he learned that Bülowius had still not broken through the pass. The attacks resumed in the early morning with heavy artillery preparation, including the new Nebelwerfer multiple rocket launchers, better known to the US troops as the "Screaming Meemies" due to their terrifying

The 10th Panzer Division captured a large number of US half-tracks of the 3/6th Armored Infantry at the base of Djebel Semmama and quickly put them back into use, as seen here. This column from Panzergrenadier Regiment 69 is on the move in Kasserine Pass with an SdKfz 263 armored command car behind it. (NARA)

A US 105mm howitzer of the 33d Field Artillery Battalion, 1st Infantry Division, provides fire support near Kasserine Pass on February 20, 1943. (MHI)

This PzKpfw IV Ausf. F2 of Panzer Battalion Stotten, Panzer Regiment 8, 15th Panzer Division was lost in Kasserine Pass. (NARA)

sound. A battalion of the 5th Bersaglieri was sent to reinforce Pz.Gren.Regt. Afrika in its fight with the 1/26th Infantry on Djebel Semmama. The 5th Bersaglieri "fought valiantly" according to the DAK diary but suffered heavy losses, including their commander.

Rommel had changed his mind about the dispositions of his attack. An initial attack towards Sbiba by the 21st Panzer Division the day before had been sharply rebuffed, suggesting that defenses along that route might already be firm. He did not realize at the time that the defenses at Sbiba were about three times the size of the German attacking force. With 10th Panzer Division still en route, the question remained whether to commit it to the Sbiba route and risk it becoming bogged down behind the 21st Panzer Division, or send it through Kasserine Pass and up the road to Thala. Rommel decided on the latter approach. The 10th Panzer Division was not at full strength and Arnim refused to release its Tiger battalion. By mid afternoon, the advance elements of the 10th Panzer Division had arrived at Kasserine Pass, including the division's motorcycle battalion and two Panzergrenadier battalions. At 1630 hours,

An Italian Semovente 47/32 tank destroyer supporting the Centauro Division in Kasserine Pass on February 23, 1943. (NARA)

Rommel inspects a Crusader of the British 26th Armoured Brigade knocked out in the defense of the road to Thala. (NARA)

five artillery battalions opened fire and a coordinated attack was launched down the middle of the pass, with infantry action continuing in the hills above. The collapse of an engineer company near the road allowed the 10th Panzer Division battlegroup to begin moving up the Thala road. Gore's blocking force managed to temporarily stop the attack, so at dusk the 1/Pz. Regt. 8 was thrown into the attack. The Panzers finally overwhelmed the British tanks as well as the five tank destroyers from the 805th Tank Destroyer Battalion reinforcing the roadblocks, and pushed a short distance up the road before darkness fell.

The American defenses had been shattered by the late-afternoon attack and Co. I, 13th Armored had lost all of its tanks in the fighting. The last unit in the German path along the road to Tebessa was the French 75mm battery, and after running out of ammunition, the gun crews spiked their weapons and retreated. Rommel exploited the initial success by sending a battalion from the Centauro Division down the Tebessa road, which reached about five miles into the pass, nearing the

Bou Chebko Pass exits by nightfall. The isolated American detachments, such as Wells' 3/6th Armored Infantry and the survivors of the 1/26th Infantry, were encircled on Djebel Semmama. The 3/6th Armored Infantry had left their half-tracks at the base of the djebel before deploying on the heights, and the Germans captured most of them intact. It was a much appreciated windfall for the German troops who were short of mechanized transport for their infantry, and they were gladly put back into service by the German troops.

Since it was now clear that the Germans were staging their attack towards Tebessa through Kasserine, Fredendall was able to shift forces blocking other passes to the Kasserine area. He ordered units of 1st Infantry Division into the hills on the southwestern side of the pass. Robinett began to move CCB/1st Armored Division into northern entrance of Kasserine Pass along the Tebessa road on the morning of February 20, and the units began arriving by the early afternoon. Fredendall originally planned to delegate responsibility for the entire defense of the pass to Robinett, but realizing the magnitude of the task, he instead divided the command, with Robinett responsible for clearing the pass south of the Hatab River, and Dunphie and the 26th Armoured Brigade north of the river. In the face of such disarray, Anderson had other ideas and sent Brig. Cameron Nicholson, assistant commander of the British 6th Armoured Division, to Thala to command all US, British and French troops in the sector under his improvised "Nickforce" command, further adding to the confusion.

Kesselring stopped in Tunis before returning to Rome on the afternoon of February 20. He had an angry meeting with Arnim, accusing him of defying his orders by holding back elements of the 10th Panzer Division. Arnim lamely replied that the units in question were at the front and difficult to disengage. Arnim also made clear his suspicions that Rommel was aiming for Tebessa, not towards Le Kef where his army was supposed to stage a diversionary attack. Kesselring reiterated his instructions to stage such an attack. Arnim grudgingly agreed, but postponed the attack until February 22. Kesselring was so angry at Arnim's

French and American infantry inspect one of the M-14/41 tanks of the Italian 131 Armored Regiment, Centauro Division lost during the fighting in Kasserine Pass. (NARA)

A Semovente M41 75/18 of Centauro Division knocked out during the Kasserine fighting. Armed with a short 75mm gun, this was the best Italian armored vehicle of the Tunisian campaign. (MHI)

A reconnaissance patrol from the 894th Tank Destroyer Battalion moves down the Thala–Kasserine road in late February 1943. (NARA)

truculence that on returning to Rome, he recommended that Rommel be put in charge of all Axis forces in Tunisia, including Arnim's 5th Panzer Army.

Rommel used the morning of February 21 to consolidate his gains in Kasserine Pass and to make certain his forces were ready for any Allied counterattack. Rommel was undecided about the ultimate objective of his attack and still tempted to press for Tebessa instead of Le Kef. To some extent, the geography helped decide the issue. The Hatab River was engorged by the winter rains, and the US engineers had destroyed the main bridge over the river. As a result, the pass was effectively divided and the two battlegroups were physically separated by the river. Rommel made no effort to consolidate his forces against a single objective, but instead accepted the existing dispersion, sending Bülowius' Kampfgruppe DAK down the road to Tebessa while Broich's 10th Panzer Division continued along a northeastern route towards Thala. Rommel's indecisiveness can be traced back to the disputes between Kesselring and the Comando Supremo over the mission of Operation *Sturmflut*, but the result was to scatter the battlegroups along three different routes, none of which was strong enough to overcome the growing Allied resistance.

The backbone of Robinett's CCB, 1st Armored Division was Lt. Col. Henry Gardiner's battle-hardened 2/13th Armored. Gardiner is seen here in front of his new M4A1 tank named Henry III, after having lost Henry II in the defense of Sbeïtla. (H. Gardiner)

The DAK advance guard, a Centauro armored battalion and 33rd Reconnaissance Battalion, finally encountered the outer defenses of CCB, the Recon Co., 13th Armored on the night of February 20/21, which held them up until daylight. At 1145 hours, Rommel ordered the entire kampfgruppe into the Kasserine Pass to break through the Djebel Hamra passes to Tebessa. Robinett's CCB deployed into the valley on the morning of February 21 with 2/13th Armored, 2/6th Armored Infantry, two self-propelled artillery battalions and elements of two tank destroyer battalions. Around 1630 hours, Panzergrenadier Regiment Afrika, supported by Panzer Battalion Stotten, collided with dug-in tanks from Gardiner's 2/13th Armored, and were repulsed by tank fire and precise artillery concentrations.

With the northern pass evidently blocked, the DAK attempted to redeploy after dark on the approaches to the southern Djebel Hamra Pass. In the darkness, Panzergrenadier Regiment Afrika took the wrong road and ended up on Hill 812, dividing the battlegroup in two. In the process, it overran one of the batteries of the 33d Field Artillery Battalion. With its forces scattered, the DAK Kampfgruppe was unable to launch any significant attack on February 22. Instead, Gen. Allen ordered 3/16th Infantry to retake Hill 812 at 1600 hours to prevent a rupture between the 1st Infantry Division and CCB. The counterattack succeeded, recapturing equipment, and pushing the lost German troops back into the valley. On the right wing, some tanks from 13th Armored Regiment assaulted the 5th Bersaglieri, which was in poor shape after heavy losses in the previous fighting; their positions near Hill 732 were overrun and the Italians were sent into headlong retreat.

The attack by the 10th Panzer Division against Dunphie's British forces holding the outer defenses of Thala was both more concentrated and successful. On February 21, about 30 tanks and 25 other armored vehicles began probing the outer defenses around noon, gradually overwhelming an initial outpost line. The main attack was launched around 1500 hours. The lightly armored Crusaders and Valentines were outgunned and outranged by the German tanks and by mid afternoon about 15 had been lost. By late afternoon, with the defenses on the verge

The British 25th Tank Brigade was equipped with the new Churchill Mk.III infantry tanks like this one, and some of these heavy tanks were sent to reinforce the threatened Sbiba sector. (MHI)

A company of the 2/16th Infantry, 1st Infantry Division is seen advancing back into Kasserine Pass on February 26 following the retreat of the DAK. (MHI)

of collapse, Dunphie called for smoke, and began to withdraw his force to the final ridge line south of Thala. The Germans followed closely, and in the dark, around 1900 hours, a German column led by a captured British Valentine tank managed to get within the British defenses before being discovered. A confused close-range mêlée ensued and the kampfgruppe of 10th Panzer Division finally overcame the last British defenders in front of Thala. The defense of the Thala road had cost Dunphie's brigade 38 tanks and 28 guns; the Germans had taken 571 prisoners. But the brigade had effectively delayed the 10th Panzer Division and their stubborn defense made Broich wary of any attempt to push into Thala after dark. The delaying action had permitted critical reinforcements to trickle in from all over the Tunisian front: an infantry company of the 2nd Hampshires, the 16/5 Lancers with some new Sherman tanks, and most importantly the divisional artillery of the newly arriving US 9th Infantry Division, which arrived after a grueling 800-mile road march. The US artillery included two 105mm howitzer battalions, a 155mm howitzer battalion, and two cannon companies with 75mm pack howitzers, a substantial addition to the Thala existing defenses' of twenty-two 25-pdr guns.

Shortly before dawn, Nicholson ordered the remnants of the 2nd Lothians to stage a suicidal attack against the German positions outside Thala. Their commander, Lt. Col. Ffrench-Blake, grimly informed his ten remaining tank crews that "we've got to go out on a forlorn hope." In bad mechanical state, only five of the tanks reached German lines around dawn, and were quickly knocked out. The 10th Panzer Division commander, Friedrich von Broich, planned to launch a February 22 attack at 0700 hours, but the sacrificial attack by the Lothians and a sudden artillery barrage by the reinforced Thala defenses derailed his plans. Broich phoned Rommel that he expected the artillery was a prelude for a counterattack and so he would shift to the defensive; Rommel agreed. Both sides engaged in artillery preparation for the rest of the morning. When no Allied attack emerged, Broich rescheduled his attack for 1600 hours. For the first time in days, Allied air power intervened. A newly completed runway permitted 117 sorties against the exposed German troops, mainly by P-38 fighters, which strafed Broich's positions mercilessly. By the end of the day, the 10th Panzer Division advance against Thala had stalled.

COMMAND DECISIONS

While Rommel had concentrated his attention on the Kasserine Pass, he had not ignored the other attack axis up towards Sbiba. The 21st Panzer Division had attacked on February 19 but almost immediately ran into a determined defensive position of the US 18th Infantry supported by tanks of the British 16/5 Lancers. Attempts by Panzer Regiment 5 to break through led to the loss of about a dozen Panzers, mainly to accurate artillery fire. What Rommel had not appreciated was that Sbiba was defended by 19th Corps with elements of three divisions, substantially outnumbering his attack force. The determined nature of the defenses along the Sbiba road convinced Rommel that a sounder approach to Sbiba would be through Kasserine Pass via Thala. The 21st Panzer Division was instructed to keep up pressure against the Allied defenses toward Sbiba, but Rommel no longer considered this the most likely avenue of attack.

Two main threats confronted the 19th Corps around Sbiba. The most serious was the threat of envelopment from behind if Thala fell. The corps could not provide defense in all directions, and it was obliged on several occasions to detach units to reinforce the Kasserine defenses. By February 21, the northern front with the 5th Panzer Army began to stir, and there were signs of offensive actions—the first hints of Arnim's long-delayed attack. The threat to Thala and pressure from the 5th Panzer Army led to a decision to withdraw from Sbiba on the night of February 22/23 to new defenses near Rohia. Yet the 21st Panzer Division did not exploit this withdrawal, as the turning point had already occurred earlier in the day at Kasserine.

By the afternoon of February 22, Rommel had to make a decision regarding future operational plans. His attacks into Kasserine Pass, although initially successful, had run up against determined resistance and had been halted. There was evidence from Luftwaffe reconnaissance that the Allies were moving in reinforcements to Thala. An attack towards Tebessa through the pass was dubious since the Allies could attack the flank from Thala. The 21st Panzer Division had never had any significant success against the Sbiba defenses, so prospects in that direction were uninspiring. Although German and Italian losses in the past week's fighting had been relatively light, the operations had consumed precious fuel and ammunition. Fuel stocks for the forward Panzer elements were down to about 125–190 miles (250–300km) of travel, ammunition stocks were low, and fuel reserves with the forces on the Mareth Line were even lower. As Arnim had argued repeatedly before the launch of these attacks, logistics were the principal limiting factor in offensive operations. Unless spectacular gains were made immediately, the prospects for a decisive strategic victory would evaporate. The Allied defenses in central Tunisia had finally begun to harden. Rommel also had to consider that Montgomery's Eighth Army would soon be ready for operations against the Mareth Line. He finally had to admit that the opportunities for any major gains through Kasserine had evaporated due to the determined Allied defense.

Kesselring visited Rommel at his forward command post in Kasserine Pass in the afternoon and found him "in a very dispirited mood … His heart was not in his task and he approached it with little confidence. I was particularly struck by his ill-concealed impatience to get back as quickly as possible and with as much unimpaired strength as possible to the (Mareth) line." They both agreed that it was time for a withdrawal, and that the remaining forces would be better spent in a spoiling attack against the Eighth Army before Montgomery was ready for his inevitable offensive. Although Kesselring was content with the tactical victory scored over the inexperienced Americans, he was still angry at the quarrelsome performance of his senior commanders, especially Arnim. He engineered a change in the Axis command structure with the approval of the Comando Supremo. All Axis forces in Tunisia would be under the control of Army Group Afrika, with Rommel as its head as of February 23. He hoped this would end the continual bickering and debate between his senior commanders. This hope was short lived, as Rommel left Tunisia on March 9 for sick leave.

Arnim's promised attack in the north on February 22 never materialized. With the British 5 Corps sending so many units to Thala, Arnim proposed a local offensive on February 26 to take advantage of the weakened British positions. The attack was hastily planned and harshly rebuffed by the British, with the attacking force losing most of its Panzers to combat action or mechanical breakdown.

The Allied command structure saw some significant changes in the final days of the Kasserine Pass battles. The confusing command structure with the Americans subordinate to Anderson's First Army, but the French in a semi-autonomous position had proven to be unwieldy except for the cooperative attitude in the field of commanders like Juin and Koeltz. At the Casablanca conference, the senior Allied leaders imposed a new command structure with General Harold Alexander taking control of the new 18th Army Group with all Allied land forces under single command. Eisenhower was still reluctant to sack Fredendall while the fighting continued, so instead he dispatched the commander of the 2d Armored Division in Morocco, the pugnacious Maj. Gen. Ernest Harmon, as an assistant corps commander to keep an eye on him.

The German withdrawal order was issued at 1415 hours on February 22 and by the next day, most of the German and Italian units had left Kasserine pass. Allied actions on February 23 were wary, still not realizing that the Germans had begun to withdraw and anticipating more attacks. The following day, units began to probe the German defenses. A fully fledged move to recapture the pass didn't take place until 0630 hours, February 25 with CCB/1st Armored Division, supported by the 16th Infantry, 1st Infantry Division moving along the southern side of the pass and the British 26th Armoured Brigade moving along the northern side. The main opponent proved to be numerous mines and booby traps, as by then, the German forces had completely withdrawn.

As the situation on the front calmed down, changes were made. Eisenhower sacked his intelligence chief, E.E. Mockler-Ferryman, whose over-reliance on Enigma had resulted in serious misjudgments about Axis intentions. Fredendall's atrocious performance inspired universal complaints from US divisional commanders, and Alexander judged his performance seriously lacking. Eisenhower shifted Gen. George S. Patton from his command of the I Armored Corps in Morocco to command of II Corps. To prevent the dispersion of US forces and the haphazard mixture of British, French and US troops, Anderson's First Army remained in command of the British Fifth Corps and the French 19 Corps, but the US II Corps remained in a semi-autonomous position directly under Alexander's 18 Army Group headquarters. In reality, the French forces were so poorly equipped that most units were pulled out of the line to begin a process of complete re-equipment and re-organization.

Two strategic initiatives were pursued by the Allies in March 1943. It was becoming increasingly evident from the Enigma decrypts that the Achilles heel of the Axis forces in Tunisia was their precarious logistical lifeline across the Mediterranean. Not only were they unable to reinforce the existing garrison, but supplies of fuel and ammunition were falling seriously short of minimal requirements. The Royal Navy accelerated efforts to interdict the Axis maritime supply chain by attacking transports and merchant vessels. The second Allied initiative was to substantially improve Allied air power in Tunisia. The Luftwaffe had continued to play a strong supporting role in operations over Tunisia due to the proximity of bases on Sicily. March 1943 saw the Allies considerably step up efforts to build forward airfields to enable the RAF and USAAF to wrest control of the air from the Germans.

Besides the command changes in the US II Corps, the main emphasis was to move the remainders of US divisions forward to create cohesive units. One of the main problems in the February fighting had been the haphazard commitment of US divisions. Not a single US division had fought as a whole, which adversely impacted their performance. The 1st Armored Division was re-equipped by stripping tanks and crews from the idle 2d Armored Division, so reaching about 80 percent strength by early March, and full strength by the middle of the month. The remainders of the 1st, 9th and 34th Infantry divisions arrived and were redeployed as integral formations.

A trio of A-20 medium bombers stage a low-level attack during the fighting around Maknassy in March 1943.

SUPPORTING MONTGOMERY: OPERATION *WOP*

In the wake of the events at Kasserine Pass, the focus of the Tunisian fighting shifted. Rommel's attention turned to the threat posed by Montgomery's Eighth Army along the Mareth Line. Rommel's last action before he left Tunisia was to launch an attack by 10th Panzer Division on March 6 against the 30 Corps near Medenine on the Eighth Army's left flank. Forewarned of the attack by Enigma decrypts, Montgomery reinforced the front with anti-tank guns and inflicted a severe setback on the Panzers. Rommel finally left Tunisia on March 9, turning over command of Army Group Afrika to his rival, Arnim. The strategic initiative was shifting to the Allies and the main US effort through March was the support of Montgomery's breakthrough operations along the Mareth Line, which began on the night of March 16/17.

The first commitment of the II Corps after the Kasserine Pass fighting was in direct support of the Mareth operation. Alexander still had little confidence in the performance of the US troops, and felt that a set of modest operations with good prospects for local tactical victories would serve the dual purpose of building up experience among the green troops and improving the shattered morale in units like the 1st Armored Division. The most fruitful operation would be to conduct an advance against the right flank of the Mareth Line by moving from Tebessa towards the sea via Gafsa. Patton saw the intention of Operation *Wop* to be much like Stonewall Jackson's at the second battle of Manassas, a flank battle to support the main corps. Kesselring was dismissive of Italian warnings of the threat to Gafsa, but Arnim remained apprehensive and planned a spoiling attack on March 19 by the Centauro Division and elements of the 21st Panzer Division. The Americans struck first.

The American corps was deployed as a shield and sword. The shield consisted of the 34th Division holding the Sbiba area and the 9th Infantry Division holding the Western Dorsals from Kasserine Pass south. The 1st Armored Division was in Kasserine Pass, and elements would debouch

OPERATION *WOP*, MARCH 16–23, 1943

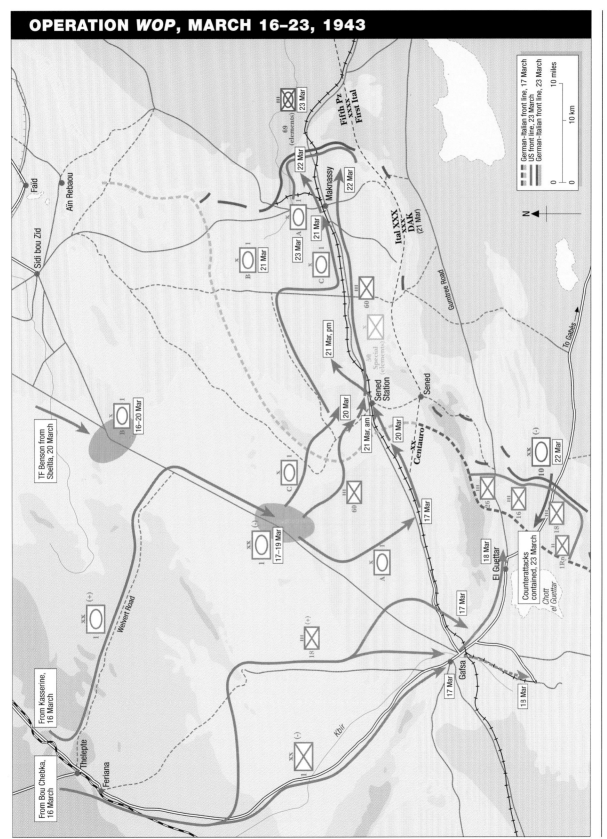

Fifth Pz. xxxx First Ital

Ital XXX xxx DAK (21 Mar)

Faid
Ain Rebaou
Sidi bou Zid
Maknassy
Guntree Road
To Gabes

23 Mar
22 Mar
22 Mar
23 Mar
21 Mar
21 Mar
23 Mar
21 Mar
69 (elements)
60
3e Special (elements)

21 Mar, pm

Sened Station
Sened

20 Mar
21 Mar, am
20 Mar

xx Centauro

TF Benson from Sbeïtla, 20 March
16–20 Mar
17–19 Mar

60
17 Mar
17 Mar

C
A

26
16
18
1Ro1

22 Mar

18 March
El Guettar
Counterattacks contained, 23 March
Chott el Guettar

From Kasserine, 16 March
From Bou Chebka, 16 March
Welvert Road
Thelepte
Feriana

18 (+)

17 Mar
17 Mar
18 Mar
Gafsa

Kbir

18

German-Italian front line, 17 March
US front line, 23 March
German-Italian front line, 23 March

0   10 miles
0   10 km

N

69

CCA, 1st Armored Division marched into Maknassy on the morning of March 22, 1943. The vehicle under the tree is an M6 37mm GMC tank destroyer. (NARA)

Two officers of the 601st Tank Destroyer Battalion discuss plans in front of their M2A1 command half-track on March 23, 1943 near El Guettar. Behind them is one of the battalion's M3 75mm GMC tank destroyers that played a critical role in the fighting that day against the 10th Panzer Division. (NARA)

from the pass and take up positions to permit operations against Gafsa from the north. The sword was Terry Allen's 1st Infantry Division and the 1st Ranger Battalion, which would move against Gafsa from the Feriana area. Axis forces in the Gafsa area were primarily two Italian infantry battalions with some tank and field artillery support. The expectation was that the garrison's mission would be to delay the US attack but that they would withdraw if confronted.

On the night of March 16/17, the 16th and 18th Infantry made a 45-mile approach march by truck, and deployed under the cover of darkness outside Gafsa. The assault was delayed until mid morning, but the US infantry overran the small security outposts and found that the garrison had withdrawn. On March 18, the 1st Rangers occupied neighboring El Guettar. After remaining at the initial objectives for a day in case of counterattack, the next stage of the operation was scheduled for March 19, an advance by the 1st Armored Division against Sened Station. This had to be postponed due to the rainy weather, resulting in overflowing streams, flooded areas and muddy roads, which made a mechanized advance

A crewman from the 601st Tank Destroyer Battalion armed with a Thompson sub-machine gun runs over to an abandoned Italian 47mm anti-tank gun position near El Guettar during the fighting there on March 23, 1943. (NARA)

Gafsa was retaken by the 1st Infantry Division on March 17, and here an American correspondent is seen recording the scene. Of interest is the GI in the center of the picture seen carrying one of the new bazooka 2.36in. anti-tank rocket launchers, first issued the previous month. (NARA)

impossible. The attack on Sened Station was made by CCA advancing along the Gafsa road, while the attached 60th Infantry from the 9th Division marched over Djebel Goussa with the support of CCC and attacked the town from the north. The garrison was overwhelmed by the unexpected maneuver, but part of the garrison escaped south to the village of Sened where they were captured on March 23. Operation *Wop* was supposed to conclude with a demonstration towards Maknassy, to threaten the German flank. However, the attack had progressed so well to date, with the Axis resistance so fleeting, that the mission was expanded to a seizure of the ridge east of Maknassy and an armored raid further east to the Mezzouna airfield. The CCA advanced on the night of March 21 to Maknassy and sent patrols into the town after dawn, finding the town abandoned of enemy troops.

The mission of the II Corps continued to expand. On March 21, Montgomery suggested to Alexander that an armored thrust by the corps along the Sfax–Gabès road threatening to cut off the Mareth defenses from the rear would aid his ongoing attack on the Mareth Line. Alexander considered such an attack a little too bold, and ordered Patton on a more limited mission of pushing the II Corps out past Maknassy and conducting raids against the German supply lines around Mahares.

As Alexander had anticipated, the advance of the II Corps worried Arnim and on March 22 he instructed Gen. Vaerst, the new commander of 5th Panzer Army, to dispatch troops from the reserve to hold the hills east of Maknassy, and to use the 10th Panzer Division to attack the US 1st Infantry Division in the Gafsa area. The most critical defense point was Hill 322, which controlled the pass exiting from Maknassy to the east. Arnim deployed a detachment from the Afrika Korps for this key position, troops that had formerly been Rommel's personal guard detachment.

The advance east from Maknassy began shortly before midnight on March 22 by 1/6th Armored Infantry and the 3/60th Infantry. The attack started after the Afrika Korps reinforcements had arrived. Although parts of the mountain passes were secured, Hill 322 proved to be tenaciously

US UNITS (BLUE)
1   Co. A, 601st Tank Destroyer Battalion
2   Co. B, 601st Tank Destroyer Battalion
3   Co. C, 601st Tank Destroyer Battalion
4   899th Tank Destroyer Battalion
13 17th Field Artillery Regiment (155mm
       howitzer)

1st Infantry Division
5   2/16th Infantry
6   3/16th Infantry
7   1/18th Infantry
8   2/18th Infantry
9   3/18th Infantry
10 26th Infantry
11 5th Field Artillery Battalion (155mm
       howitzer)
12 32d Field Artillery Battalion (105mm
       howitzer)

1st

EL GUETTAR

GUMTREE ROAD

CHOTT EL GUETTAR
SALT MARSH

HILL 3

DJEBEL BERDA

B

▼ EVENTS

1. **18th Infantry overcomes Centauro Division defenses along Gabès road by March 22.**

2. **26th Infantry proceeds along Gumtree Road against Italian defenses.**

3. **Kampfgruppe 10th Panzer Division begins moving up Gabès road around 0500 hours, conducting reconnaissance by fire against 18th Infantry positions on Djebel el Mcheltat.**

4. **A Panzergrenadier detachment moves off on foot around dawn, securing part of Djebel Kreroua for DAK command post.**

5. **Other Panzergrenadier detachments split off from main body, one moving into foothills of Djebel el Mcheltat and the other south against US positions on Djebel Berda.**

6. **Main attack forms up in early morning with two battalions from Panzer Regiment 7 in front, and Panzergrenadiers moving behind in a slow assault up the Gabès road towards El Guettar.**

7. **German attack slowed by tank destroyers but fights into US artillery emplacements at base of Hill 336. German assault is stymied during close-range fighting with tank destroyers, artillery and 16th Infantry.**

8. **German Panzer detachment continues towards El Guettar, a few Panzers get stuck in Chott el Guettar salt marsh to the west.**

9. **Reinforcements begin arriving from II Corps, including 899th Tank Destroyer Battalion (M10 3in. GMC), which halts lead Panzers at a cost of seven tank destroyers.**

10. **3/16th Infantry moves forward from positions along Gumtree Road to reinforce 2/16th Infantry.**

11. **Co. E, 2/16th Infantry stages limited counterattack against German infantry moving into foothills below Hill 483.**

12. **Additional reinforcements arrive from II Corps, including elements of 17th Field Artillery Regiment.**

13. **Kampfgruppe withdraws about noon.**

14. **Kampfgruppe begins another attack around 1645 hours, but is shattered by artillery, and begins retreating around 1845 hours.**

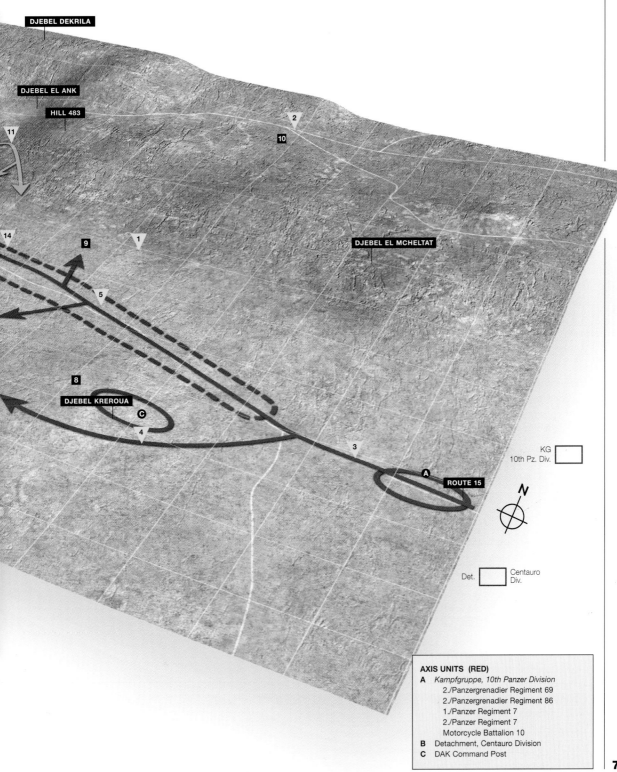

EL GUETTAR, MARCH 23, 1943
The US Army's first victory over the Wehrmacht.

Note: the gridlines are at intervals of 1 mile.

DJEBEL DEKRILA

DJEBEL EL ANK

HILL 483

11

2

10

14

9

1

DJEBEL EL MCHELTAT

5

8

DJEBEL KREROUA

C

4

3

A

ROUTE 15

KG
10th Pz. Div.

N

Det.

Centauro
Div.

AXIS UNITS (RED)

A *Kampfgruppe, 10th Panzer Division*
       2./Panzergrenadier Regiment 69
       2./Panzergrenadier Regiment 86
       1./Panzer Regiment 7
       2./Panzer Regiment 7
       Motorcycle Battalion 10
B Detachment, Centauro Division
C DAK Command Post

defended and several infantry attacks were beaten off. Later attacks, even with artillery and tank support failed on March 23 and the Afrika Korps was able to reinforce the hill defenses with Kampfgruppe Lang. Patton was so aggravated by the delay that he ordered Gen. Ward to personally lead the next day's attack. Although the attack on the morning of March 25 by the 6th Armored Infantry succeeded in gaining part of the hill, German artillery fire forced the Americans to abandon their gains. Patton's attention was soon diverted to the southwest.

The 1st Infantry Division had continued to advance out of El Guettar on March 20 against positions of the Italian Centauro Division into the valley along the Gafsa–Sfax road. The division's regiments were separated by the numerous hills, with the 26th Infantry operating along the Gumtree Road towards Sfax. Before dawn on the morning of March 23, a kampfgruppe of the 10th Panzer Division began moving up along the Gabès–Gafsa road between the positions of the 16th and 18th Infantry. The German attack consisted of Panzers and Panzergrenadiers in half-tracks, moving methodically along the road at daylight, followed by more infantry on trucks. Since the 1st Infantry Division was in the process of moving forward itself along the hills on either side of the valley, there were no defenses in the valley itself to interfere with the advancing German column. The German spearhead was first engaged by the 601st Tank Destroyer Battalion deployed in front of the divisional artillery, and by intense, close-range artillery fire. The tank destroyers managed to slow but not stop the attack, and the German attack broke into the emplacements of the two field artillery battalions before grinding to a halt. Losses had been so heavy that the German kampfgruppe withdrew two miles to regroup behind a ridgeline to await preparatory bombardment of the US positions by Stukas. The attack resumed in the late afternoon around 1645 hours, but the Stukas had accomplished little and the delay had permitted the US forces in the area to regroup. The renewed attack faltered almost at once. The 18th Infantry report after the battle noted: "Our artillery crucified them and they were falling like flies." Following the failed attack and heavy losses of March 23, the 10th Panzer Division was no longer in a position to undertake offensive actions against the 1st Infantry Division, but managed to prevent its advance. The victory at El Guettar substantially

The Luftwaffe remained a major threat through most of the March fighting. This 40mm M1 anti-aircraft gun was deployed near El Guettar on March 23, 1943. (MHI)

Troops lay communication wire to forward positions as tanks of the 1st Armored Division move forward in Bir Mrabot Pass during the fighting southeast of El Guettar. (MHI)

boosted American morale and made it clear to Arnim that the US Army was already improving since the easy victories at Kasserine.

Alexander's growing confidence in the II Corps, and the helpful results of its actions in support of Montgomery's offensive along the Mareth Line, led to plans for more ambitious operations on March 25. The drive past Maknassy had proven futile due to the German defenses in the pass, so instead, the 1st Armored Division would reinforce a drive from El Guettar towards Gabès. In addition, the 9th and 34th Divisions were relieved of their defensive missions, and the 34th Division assigned to push through one of the passes in the Eastern Dorsals at Fondouk el Aoureb, while the 9th Division would assist in the attack towards Gabès.

The attack began on March 28–29 with opening moves by the 9th Division on the southern flank of the II Corps lines. The infantry advance was frustrated by the extremely rough terrain, and by determined resistance from well-entrenched Italian troops in the rocky hills. The slow advance meant that the 9th Division was not in position for its main push until April 1–2. The 1st Infantry Division advanced

10TH PANZER DIVISION AT EL GUETTAR;
DAWN, MARCH 23, 1943 (pp 76–77)
Before dawn on the morning of March 23, 1943
a kampfgruppe of the 10th Panzer Division made a rapid
road march up Route 15 into the valley approaching El
Guettar. Tanks of Panzer Regiment 7, such as the PzKpfw IV
Ausf. G (1), led the columns, while Panzergrenadiers in
SdKfz 251 half-tracks, captured M3 half-tracks, and various
trucks followed behind (2). Around dawn, the lead tanks
began conducting "reconnaissance by fire" against the
slopes on either side of the road, firing machine guns into
areas where American troops might be deployed. There was
little response from the 18th Infantry, which was deployed
in trenches well up in the foothills. As a result, the
kampfgruppe continued up Route 15 unmolested. Later in
the morning, when US artillery began to fall on the column,
it began its battle deployment. The Panzers formed an outer
cordon, with the dismounted infantry advancing behind
them. An American officer in the hills above thought it
looked like "a huge iron fort moving down the valley." By
this time, the 10th Panzer Division had been reduced to
a strength of 57 tanks—having started the campaign a few
months earlier with 159, including 21 PzKpfw II, 114 PzKpfw
III and 24 PzKpfw IV. Only 16 of these Panzers were the
PzKpfw IV Ausf. G with the long 75mm gun, the type most
similar to the American M4 medium tank, and the type
shown here in the vanguard of the attack. German tank
tactics in the desert mirrored the slow movement of a wary
hunter, not the bold charge of cavalry. This stirred up less
dust, making the tanks less conspicuous targets. In

addition, it prevented the dust clouds from obscuring the
vision of Panzers and Panzergrenadiers behind the initial
attack wave. On the negative side, a slow advance under
artillery fire was a harrowing experience for the
Panzergrenadiers and potentially a very costly tactic,
as the fighting this day would prove. Against little
opposition, the "iron wall" of Panzers moved relentlessly
up the valley until it came within range of the 75mm guns
on the half-track tank destroyers of the 601st Tank
Destroyer Battalion, arrayed in a cordon around two
battalions of the 1st Infantry Division's field artilery.
The 601st inflicted considerable damage on the Panzers,
claiming to have knocked out 30 at a cost of 21 of their
own tank destroyers. The battalion was also instrumental in
blunting the German infantry attack, adding to the firepower
of the artillery battalions with high-explosive ammunition
and machine gun fire. Despite the high volume of fire, the
"iron fort" crashed into the American artillery positions
before finally being stopped by the arrival of reinforcements.
The kampfgruppe retreated down the valley in the early
afternoon to rally its bloodied troops. A renewed attack was
launched at dusk, but with far less Panzer support due
to the earlier losses. The German infantry was mown down
by artillery and machine gun fire without reaching the US
positions. George Patton, who witnessed the second attack,
remarked: "My god, it seems a crime to murder good
infantry like that." By the end of the day, the 10th Panzer
Division was down to 26 serviceable tanks, and a later
report to higher headquarters indicated that the division
was "in dire straits" after the attack.

more quickly across open ground, though at the disadvantage of being exposed to German observation and artillery fire. The advance slowed as two of its regiments penetrated into the hill mass of Djebel el Mcheltat. With the operations of the 34th Infantry Division around Fondouk not having the desired results, Alexander instructed Patton to step up the II Corps attack towards Gabès to keep the Axis forces off balance while Montgomery's Eighth Army prepared to assault the next Axis defensive line along the Chott Position. Patton decided to use an armored task force of the 1st Armored Division led by Col. Clarence Benson. Since the front with the Eighth Army had calmed down, Arnim was able to reinforce the El Guettar front with additional units including most of the 21st Panzer Division and Panzergrenadier Regiment Afrika.

The initial attack by TF Benson at noon on March 30 was stymied by a minefield in the pass between Djebel Mcheltat and Hill 369. A broader attack the following day with support by the infantry on either side made modest gains but German anti-tank positions prevented any deep penetration into the valley, and the Luftwaffe was particularly active with 151 sorties. The following day, a diversionary attack was attempted by CCA near Maknassy but with little effect. Alexander changed the plans again, instructing Patton to emphasize an infantry assault before the armor penetration. Patton was especially critical of the poor performance of Allied air support over the II Corps sector, and as if to stress the point, the Luftwaffe bombed near Patton's headquarters on the day that the air force senior commanders were visiting Patton to discuss the problem.

The fighting over the next few days comprised an intense infantry skirmish in the hilly country on either side of the Gabès road, with both sides suffering significant casualties in the process. Patton was not happy about the direction of the 1st Armored Division and replaced Ward with Ernest Harmon of the 2d Armored Division.

By the evening of April 6, the battle for the Chott Position by Montgomery's Eighth Army had reached a critical phase, so Alexander ordered Patton to stage a broad frontal assault the next day, no matter the number of casualties, in the hope of affecting the outcome. In fact, the Germans had predicted the likely outcome of the fighting and had already begun to withdraw their forces out of the hills under the cover of a heavy artillery bombardment that night. When the US forces began to move on the morning of April 7, they encountered little resistance and Patton began pushing TF Benson forward. The lead elements of Benson's force met up with a British reconnaissance detachment near Sebkret en Noual. This marked the end of II Corps operations in south-central Tunisia and a new phase in the Tunisian campaign for the US Army.

The one exception to this was the 34th Division, which had been committed to support a British First Army attack on the Fondouk–Pichon passes. The first series of attacks starting on March 27 were stymied by defenses in the hills on the south side of the pass, and Alexander realized that he had committed too small a force for such extensive defenses. A second attempt was made by the 34th Division to the south, and elements of the French 19th Corps and British 9 Corps to the north on April 8. The first day's fighting was frustrating on account of determined German resistance and confusion when tanks from the British 6th Armoured Division were squeezed into the 34th Division sector without coordination.

The British armored thrust was halted by extensive minefields in the passes, but the capture of the Djebel Ain el Rhorab in the British sector threatened to undermine the German defenses. British armor began to squeeze through the minefields in the pass along the sector boundary between 9 Corps and the 34th Division, leading to some combined US–British actions during the fighting on April 9. The determined German defense of the passes was due to the need to keep them blocked at least until April 10 to cover the flank of the Axis forces retreating from the Chott Position. Had the British 9 Corps been able to make it through the passes to Kairouan, a portion of the Axis forces might have been trapped. The German defenders continued to tenaciously guard the passes, and the British 6th Armoured Division did not manage to exit the Fondouk el Aoureb gap until 1000 hours on April 10, too late to interfere with the Axis retreat in any significant way.

The failure to penetrate the Fondouk–Pichon passes in time led to a great deal of recrimination between British and American officers. The 9 Corps commander, Gen. John Crocker, blamed poor training of the 34th Division for the failure to clear the passes expeditiously, but American officers complained about the poor corps plan of attack. Eisenhower and Alexander quickly stepped in to halt the arguments, and the 34th Division was put through a rigorous retraining operation. But the recriminations had taken their toll on British–American relations, affecting later operations.

THE FINAL CAMPAIGN IN TUNISIA

The Axis retreat from the Chott Position in mid April consolidated the two main Axis groupings, 5th Panzer Army and the 1st Italian Army, in the northern Tunisian bridgehead. Eisenhower suggested that the main blow against the bridgehead be directed by Anderson's First Army, since it was in the best position to conduct the operation, and had not enjoyed the limelight afforded the Eighth Army since its decisive victories at El Alamein and the Mareth Line. Eisenhower also made it clear to Alexander that he wanted the US II Corps in the fight. Alexander's initial plan subordinated II Corps to Anderson's First Army. Patton

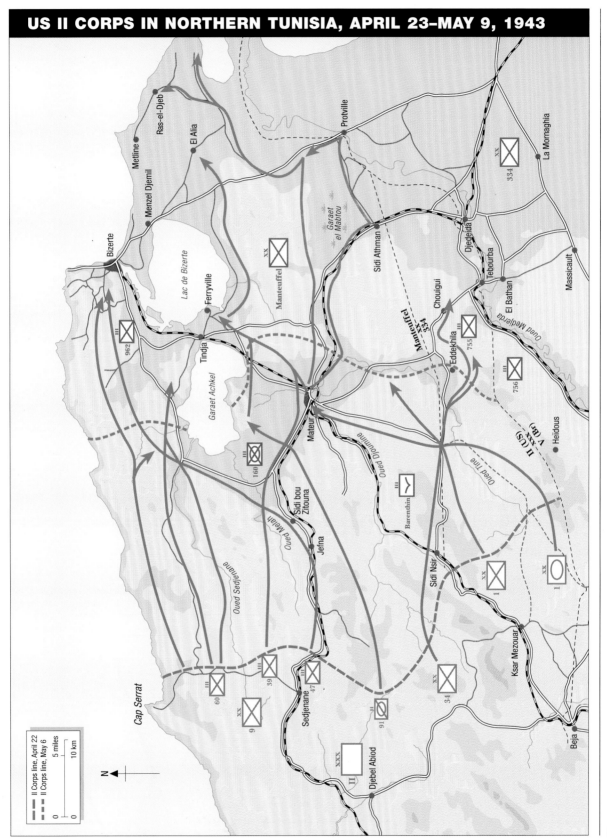

Ras-el-Djeb
Metline
El Alia
Menzel Djemil
Protville
La Mornaghia
XX
334
Bizerte
Manteuffel
XX
Garaet
el Mabtou
Lac de Bizerte
Sidi Athman
Djedeïda
Tebourba
Ferryville
Chouïgui
El Bathan
Massicault
III
962
Tindja
Manteuffel
XX
334
Eddekhila
XX
755
Oued Medjerda
III
756
Mateur
III
160
Heïdous
XXX
V (Br)
II (US)
Garaet Achkel
Oued Douïmine
Oued Tine
Sidi bou
Zitouna
III
Barenthin
Jefna
XX
1
Sidi Nsir
XX
334
Oued Melah
Ksar Mezouar
Béja
Oued Sedjenane
Cap Serrat
III
60
III
39
Sedjenane
III
47
XX
91
XX
9
Djebel Abiod
XXX
II

II Corps line, April 22
II Corps line, May 6
0   5 miles
0   10 km

N

Hill 609 posed a substantial obstacle to the advance of the 34th Division due to its rugged escarpments evident here. German artillery observers helped the Wehrmacht control the neighboring terrain from perches above, and it took four costly attacks before it was finally captured on April 30. (NARA)

strongly objected to the plan, arguing that there was still a lot of ill will after 9 Corps blamed the 34th Division for the failure at Fondouk, and the dismissive attitude of the British staff towards the 1st Armored Division. As a result, the US II Corps was shifted to the far north of the Allied line, and left directly under Alexander's 18 Army Group command rather than under Anderson's control.

In preparation for the final campaign, the Allied air forces had initiated the long delayed Operation *Flax* on April 5, aimed at strangling Axis air supply into the Tunisian bridgehead. Fighter sweeps were conducted off the Tunisian coast to catch German and Italian transports as they flew into

A motorized column from the 34th Division led by an M2 half-track approaches Mateur on May 5, 1943. (NARA)

A patrol of the 60th Infantry, 9th Division on the hills approaching Bizerte on May 7, 1943. (NARA)

The road to Mateur was littered with destroyed German equipment including this PzKpfw III Ausf. N in the foreground, a turretless Tiger in the center, and a PzKpfw IV to the extreme right. (NARA)

Tunisia, and US B-17 bombers were used to attack Axis airfields to catch transports on the ground. By the end of April, the air operations had been so successful that the Luftwaffe restricted air flights into Tunisia to individual night missions instead of massed day formations.

The crisis in Tunisia led Mussolini to suggest to Hitler that a truce be obtained with the Soviet Union so that the Axis could concentrate on defending Tunisia and prevent the Allies from leap-frogging to Italy. Mussolini correctly assumed that the Allies were planning to use North Africa as a base of operations for later campaigns. Hitler rejected this notion, and argued that the Tunisian bridgehead could be held indefinitely in an "African Verdun" due to the quality of the troops and the difficult terrain. A major resupply effort by sea and air was promised, even though supplies through March and early April had been far below requirements.

The US planning for the II Corps attack was conducted mainly by Gen. Omar Bradley, a West Point classmate of Eisenhower's who had been brought to Tunisia to act as Ike's aide, but who was "poached" by Patton when he was assigned to command II Corps. When Patton was shifted to command Seventh Army in mid April for the anticipated invasion of Sicily, Bradley took his place at the head of II Corps.

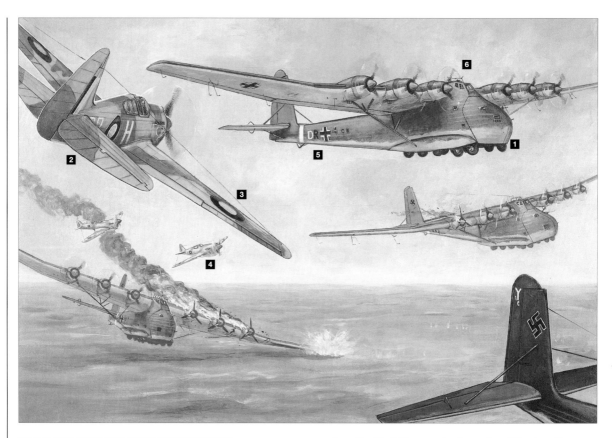

OPERATION *FLAX*: THE CAPE BON MASSACRE
APRIL 22, 1943 (pp 84–85)

By April, the supply situation for Army Group Afrika had reached a critical point as the sea routes grew increasingly dangerous for Axis shipping. Vital supplies were moved by air, but this avenue too was being choked off by the Allies' Operation *Flax*, which started on April 5, 1943. Allied successes quickly mounted. On April 5, a patrol comprising twenty-six US P-38 Lightning fighters caught a transport mission of some sixty Ju-52 transports with about two dozen escort fighters northeast of Cape Bon, and shot down eleven transports and five other aircraft. The tally quickly increased: April 10 saw the loss of 20 transports and 8 fighters; April 11 saw the loss of 26 transports and 5 fighters. Worse was yet to come. On Palm Sunday, April 18, Allied fighters attacked a huge air convoy off Cape Bon, claiming one hundred Ju-52 transports and sixteen escort fighters for the loss of seven Allied fighters. But the desperate supply situation of Army Group Afrika warranted desperate measures, and another aerial convoy was scheduled for Holy Thursday, April 22. This time, the pilots were told to stay away from Cape Bon. The April 22 mission included ten Ju-52 transports of Kampfgruppe z.b.V. 106 and 15 of the enormous Me-323 Gigant heavy transports (1) of Kampfgruppe z.b.V. 323 from Pomigliano airbase in Italy. One Me-323 crashed on take off, but the remainder headed for Cape Farina, Tunisia with an escort of thirty-nine Bf-109 fighters around 0830 hours. For reasons that remain

unclear, the Me-323 group leader ordered his aircraft to separate from the Ju-52 squadrons about halfway to the objective, and headed towards Cape Bon with a much reduced escort of fighters. The Gigant formation reached the area between Cape Bon and Zembra Island around 0925 hours and immediately encountered Allied fighters consisting of two squadrons of RAF Spitfires and four squadrons of South African Air Force P-40 Kittyhawks (2), distinguished by the orange colour of their markings (such as the roundels, (3) and the SAAF Wing emblems on the nose (4). The numerous Allied fighters quickly separated the escorts from the transports, and the Kittyhawks began a series of relentless attacks against the huge and vulnerable Me-323s, which were flying quite low to the water. Fully loaded with over 700 drums of fuel and tons of ammunition, the Gigant transports became enormous fireballs when attacked. A total of 13 Gigants were shot down by South Africans of No. 4 and No. 5 squadrons, and the one escaping Gigant was trailed by a RAF Spitfire of No. 260 Squadron and shot down. After the Holy Thursday massacre, as it became known, Luftwaffe transport missions were limited to night flights and air supply for the trapped German forces in Tunisia was effectively halted. The Me-323 in the upper portion of the illustration bears the markings of 6. Stafell, II Gruppe (5). Note also the He-111-style machine gun position above the cockpit too (6); this modification was introduced for added defense in the Tunisian theater.

Alexander's plan was to use II Corps to cover the flank of the British 5 Corps as it advanced along the Medjerda River. The II Corps contained all four US divisions employed earlier—the 1st Armored, 1st, 9th and 34th Infantry Divisions—as well as the regiment-sized Corps Franc d'Afrique. The principal Axis force opposing the II Corps was Division von Manteuffel, an improvized formation with about nine battalion-sized units numbering 5,000 troops, a quarter of whom were Italian Bersaglieri or marines. Although substantially outnumbered, Manteuffel's troops enjoyed the advantage of excellent defensive positions dug out of the rocky hills during the past several months of fighting in this sector.

The attacks began on a broad front on April 23 with the 9th Infantry Division on the left (northern) flank pushing into the mountains along the coast while the 1st Infantry Division pushed into the hills leading towards the Tine River valley. The fighting was extremely difficult due to the terrain and the prepared German defenses, but progress was gradually made. The 34th Division in the center had little success in budging Barenthin's paratrooper force on Hill 609, the dominant terrain position in this hilly sector. Bradley held the 1st Armored Division in reserve as the terrain did not favor its use, and he planned to use it to best effect once the infantry had won passage to the coastal plains.

The fighting in the 34th and 1st Divisions' sectors continued to be shaped by the need to take Hill 609 and the surrounding hills. During the final days of April, tanks were brought in to assist the assault and on April 30, Hills 609, 531 and 523 were finally seized. Hill 523 proved to be the most difficult; it was seized by 1/16th Infantry after dark on the night of April 29/30. The summit was exposed rock and vulnerable to

Gen. Willibald Borowietz, commander of the 15th Panzer Division and two other generals negotiated the surrender of Wehrmacht forces around Bizerte with Gen. Ernest Harmon, commander of the 1st Armored Division. (MHI)

fire from German positions on neighboring hills. A German counterattack overwhelmed the battalion, captured the commander and 150 men and killed the rest. The arrival of an American tank company prevented the Germans from holding on to the hill, but neither side had the strength to keep it under their control after the bitter fighting. The US hold on the other two hills was precarious, and the US defenses were subjected to repeated counterattacks. But by May 1, the US positions on Hill 609 had been reinforced, providing excellent visibility of German defenses, and permitting excellent fire control of US artillery on all subsequent German counterattacks. This broke the back of German defenses in the sector.

In the meantime, the 9th Infantry Division had pushed German defenders along the coast back into the hills approaching Bizerte exposing the defenses of Panzergrenadier Regiment 160 to possible envelopment along the coast of the Garaet Ichkul Lake. In combination with the advances in front of Mateur, Manteuffel realized that his main defenses were on the verge of envelopment. The 5th Panzer Army ordered a withdrawal back to prepared positions on either side of Garaet Ichkuel Lake on the nights of May 2 and 3. Mateur was abandoned on May 2 and CCB/1st Armored Division began a pursuit of withdrawing German units on May 3, reaching the city and capturing a few stragglers. It was evident from reconnaissance that the Germans had reinforced the hills leading to Bizerte with anti-tank guns, so the combat command took up positions near the city to prevent a German counterattack, and to permit follow-up forces to arrive.

Infantry of the 9th Division warily advance into Bizerte behind an M3 medium tank of the 751st Tank Battalion on May 7, 1943. (NARA)

The final attack towards Bizerte was scheduled to coincide with the other 18 Army Group efforts against Tunis and Cape Bon. Beginning on May 6, the 9th Division pressed in on Bizerte from north of Garet Ichkuel and seized the dominating height, Djebel Cheniti. This permitted supporting armored units such as the 751st Tank Battalion to begin probing forward towards Bizerte on May 7. Tanks pushed into the city later in the day and found that the Germans had abandoned the city without a fight, moving across to the peninsula east of Bizerte Lake. Corps Franc d'Afrique was brought by truck to Bizerte on May 8 to be given the honor of liberating the city.

The rest of II Corps renewed their attacks beyond Mateur on May 6, with the 1st Armored Division pushing up the road towards Ferryville. Although anti-tank guns knocked out over a dozen tanks in the initial assault, by May 7 Ferryville had been cut off. By this stage, Manteuffel's troops had been pocketed in three main groups around Bizerte Lake, east of the Tine River, and to the northwest of Tunis. The Axis forces were suffering from severe shortages of supplies and ammunition, and it was becoming increasingly clear that they were surrounded with little hope of reinforcement or evacuation. Nevertheless, there were still formidable defenses around Bizerte, including extensive coastal
batteries and Flak positions.

A task force under Lt. Col. Frank Carr consisting of the 1/13th Armored and 3/6th Armored Infantry moved out on the afternoon of May 7 to cut off the German forces on the east side of the Bizerte Lake. A light tank column raced ahead on May 8, subjected to fire from emplaced 105mm Flak guns that knocked out six tanks. But by the early morning hours of May 9, TF Carr had reached the Mediterranean coast.

The German collapse in northern Tunisia occurred quickly due to the obvious hopelessness of the situation and the exhaustion of the troops. Gen. von Vaerst, commander of the 5th Panzer Army, reported to Armin on the morning of May 9 that "our armor and artillery have been destroyed; we are without ammunition and fuel; we shall fight to the last." In fact, Vaerst had sent emissaries to the American lines to discuss surrender, and terms were reached with Gen. Harmon later in the morning. The 10th and 15th Panzer Division surrendered at 1250 hours on March 9. The Göring Reconnaissance Battalion held out in caves on the Djebel Ichkuel, but eventually some 40,000 troops surrendered to the II Corps. German forces in the south facing the British First Army surrendered by May 13, 1943. In the end, some 272,000 Axis troops surrendered, a total rivaling Stalingrad—leading some newspapers to dub the victory "Tunisgrad."

The roads around Bizerte were littered with wrecks and abandoned German equipment, such as this PzKpfw III Ausf. L. (Patton Museum)

THE CAMPAIGN IN RETROSPECT

Was Kasserine Pass Rommel's last victory? The attack that precipitated the Kasserine Pass battle at Sidi bou Zid was certainly a tactical victory, but it was waged by forces other than Rommel's. Rommel's main initiative was to exploit Arnim's gains at Sidi bou Zid and Sbeïtla by pushing through Kasserine Pass. Although Rommel did crack the initial defenses of Kasserine Pass on February 21, his forces never managed to break through the pass because of the American and British defenses, and he was forced to withdraw due to dwindling resources, much as his rival Arnim had predicted. The long-term advantages of the February attacks are debatable. Neither Eisenhower nor Anderson had any immediate plans to conduct major operations in central Tunisia until spring prior to the Faïd–Kasserine battles, and if anything the defeats at Kasserine encouraged the US II Corps under Patton to adopt a more aggressive posture in the forthcoming Mareth Line fighting as a means of redeeming the US Army's tarnished reputation. Contrary to the popular image, Kasserine Pass was in the end an Allied victory.

Defeat shapes an army's future—breaking the unredeemable, trapping the mediocre in recrimination, whilst spurring the fortunate to reform. The US Army was fortunate in suffering a defeat when and where it did. The Tunisian campaign was a secondary effort in a peripheral theater, involving a small force, with little strategic consequence. It occurred over a year before the main campaign in the European theater in June 1944, and thus provided the US Army with the time necessary to undergo reform. This process began almost immediately in the fields of command, doctrine, organization, and equipment. The Tunisian campaign helped to identify many of the key leaders for future campaigns. Eisenhower's leadership had been far from flawless, but his leadership skills under adversity were clear. Bradley, an unknown divisional commander prior to Kasserine, was earmarked for a rapid rise to the post of senior US tactical commander. Patton was another shining star, but whose rambunctious personality would raise questions in Sicily. On the British side, Anderson's performance had been poor and he was sidelined after Tunisia.

US Army doctrine was extensively rewritten after Tunisia. Out went fanciful ideas, and in came more practical plans for future combat based on hard-learned lessons from Tunisia. A great deal of Army doctrine was found to be sound, but training was often unrealistic and hasty. The reform was not deep enough in some areas, notably the retention of the flawed tank destroyer concept and the sluggish recognition of the need for training tank battalions to support the infantry. This was due to the Army Ground Forces bureaucracy in Washington, not the commanders in Europe. Air support doctrine saw some of the most extensive reform, with young commanders like Pete Quesada adopting the lessons taught by Air Marshal Arthur Conigham of the British Desert Air Force. This would come to fruition in the campaigns in France in 1944.

Organizational changes were swift but limited. Infantry reorganization was not as extensive as that of the armored divisions and stayed much the same, with many small improvements rather than major alterations. The armored divisions were completely reorganized, switching from a tank-heavy configuration with six tank battalions and only three infantry battalions to a better balanced, combined-arms approach with three battalions each of tanks, infantry and artillery. Equipment changes were modest, largely due to the assessment that the problems in Tunisia were due more to training, doctrine, and organization than to problems with hardware. The 37mm anti-tank gun was replaced by a mixture of bazookas and the 57mm gun. Light tanks lost their central role in armored doctrine but remained in smaller numbers for secondary roles. The M3 medium tank and M3 light tank were dropped from service in favor of the newer M5A1 light tank and M4 medium tank.

At a strategic level, the senior US leadership reverted back to "Black Jack" Pershing's dictum from World War I: US troops would fight under US commanders in US formations. After the muddle of the Tunisia campaign with intermixed British and French troops, the US Army in the European theater became very averse to deploying US troops at any level lower than army under British command. There were simply too many differences in command style and tactical doctrine for US units to operate comfortably under British command at corps and divisional level. There would be exceptions, but in general the US Army after Kasserine remained under US Army command at least an army in size—

The Allied victory parade in Tunis in June 1943 as a French colonial cavalry unit advances in review. The tank in the lower left foreground is a Somua S-35 of the 12th RCA, which took part in the Tunisia fighting. (NARA)

Patton's Seventh Army in Sicily, Clark's Fifth Army in Italy, and Bradley's First Army in Normandy.

For the Wehrmacht, the North African campaign was the high-water mark before the long slide to oblivion. The German Army still maintained a tactical and technical edge over the Allies, but the defeat in Tunisia marked the loss of the strategic initiative in the west; from May 1943 onward, Germany was on the strategic defensive. The British Army was nearing the peak of a long climb towards tactical parity with the Wehrmacht, as the Wehrmacht had begun its downward spiral. The US Army was proving to be a fast learner, and its deep modernization in artillery firepower and air power would give it the tactical edge in 1944. The command and control problems in the Wehrmacht so evident in the Tunisian campaign would only worsen. Hitler's refusal to permit a timely evacuation of Axis forces from Tunisia was the first of many such wasteful fits of pique. Hitler's feudal leadership style—a constellation of favorites all vying for the Führer's personal approval—would continue to confuse and confound effective German command leadership. In the tactical setting, the reverses of 1943 undermined Hitler's confidence in the Wehrmacht's officers, encouraging him to expand his alternative, politicized, military arm: the Waffen-SS. This only served to further complicate an already Byzantine tactical command structure.

The defeat of the Italian Army in Tunisia, combined with the enormous losses suffered in the Stalingrad campaign, marked the end of any serious role of the Italian armed forces in Axis war planning. By the time the Allies invaded Sicily on July 10, 1943 the Wehrmacht regarded the Italians as little more than cannon fodder, with the major responsibilities given to German units. The loss of Sicily in July 1943, so soon after the Libyan and Tunisian disasters, led to Mussolini's downfall and Italy's withdrawal from the Axis.

Order Date: 21/03/2020

Marketplace Order #: 202-5936505-9949122
Marketplace: Amazon UK
Customer Name: Mr Harry Butler

Order Number: 12484668

Qty Item

Kasserine Pass 1943: Rommel's last victory (Campaign)
Zaloga, Steven J.

1   SKU: wbb0013468189   W6 -1-13-012-002-3015   Good   £6.64
     ISBN: 1841769142 - Books

Notes:

Subtotal: £6.64
Shipping: £2.80
Total: £9.44

Thanks for your order!

We value our customer feedback and we want to make sure you're happy. If you're pleased with your order and the service we provided, can we ask you to leave positive feedback on the marketplace? If you are unhappy for any reason at all, please contact us at sales@webuybooks.co.uk and give us the opportunity to put it right for you. We can't fix it if we don't know about it.

Thanks again for your order and we hope to see your custom again at WeBuyBooks.

WeBuyBooks   sales@webuybooks.co.uk   www.webuybooks.co.uk

Unit 11 Hugh Business Park, Bacup Road, Waterfoot, Lancashire, BB4 7BT, UK

Margin scheme second-hand goods VAT Number GB 901 5786 27

THE BATTLEFIELDS TODAY

The fight for Tunisia in 1943 has little resonance in the Tunisian community today, and little effort has been made to preserve the memory of the events. A prominent site is the North Africa American Cemetery in Tunis, which bears witness to the sacrifices of US troops in Tunisia. The battlefields described here are in the remote desert away from the more heavily populated coastline, and the amenities that greet tourists to European battlefields are non-existent here. Recent visitors to the major battlefields such as Kasserine Pass, Sidi bou Zid, and El Guettar report that there is little significant evidence of the fighting, such as wrecked tanks or weapons. There are still some fading remnants such as shell casings, shrapnel, trenches and defensive positions in some of the more remote hills. The British monuments at Thala and Hill 609 have had their plaques removed and are bare obelisks. Some of the battlefields have changed with time—a new dam near Fondouk, better roads in the Kasserine area, the enlargement of the town of Sidi bou Zid have all contributed to this.

There are some preserved examples of weapons from the Tunisian battlefield in more accessible locations, including two Tiger I heavy tanks from the campaign. One is at the Tank Museum at Bovington in the UK, and the other was at Aberdeen Proving Ground (APG), Maryland for many years but is currently in the UK for restoration. Several of the weapons preserved at the Ordnance Museum at APG come from the Tunisia campaign including the PzKpfw II light tank, PzKpfw III Ausf. L, PzKpfw III Ausf. N, and PzKpfw IV Ausf. G medium tanks. A PzKpfw III Ausf. M tank that was at a German cemetery in Tunisia for many years was shipped back to Germany in the 1990s for restoration, and is currently in the collection at Münster.

FURTHER READING

Howe's account of the US Army in North Africa in the official US Army "Green Book" series remains the essential starting point for those interested in further details of the Kasserine campaign. There are several other books that merit special attention, including such recent titles as the Atkinson and Rolf books, as well as classics like the Blumenson book listed below. There are a surprising number of autobiographies touching on this campaign, notably the Harmon, Robinett and Kesselring accounts. For those interested in documentary sources, the US Army's Center for Military History have prepared an invaluable collection of American and German documents entitled "Kasserine Pass Battles" which is available via their website. The US Military History Institute has an interesting collection of personal records including those of generals Ward and Robinett. The National Archives and Records Administration (NARA) at College Park, Maryland is the repository for US unit records, and the author found the II Corps and 1st Armored Division records in RG 407 to be especially useful.

Atkinson, Rick *An Army at Dawn: The War in North Africa 1942–43* (Holt, 2002)
Blumenson, Martin *Kasserine Pass: Rommel's Bloody, Climactic Battle for Tunisia* (Houghton Mifflin, 1966)
Harmon, Ernest *Combat Commander* (Prentice Hall, 1970)
Hougen, John *The Story of the Famous 34th Infantry Division* (Battery Press, 1979)
Howe, George *The US Army in World War II—Northwest Africa: Seizing the Initiative in the West* (GPO, 1957)
Howe, George *The Battle History of the 1st Armored Division* (Battery Press, 1979)
Kelly, Orr *Meeting the Fox: From Operation Torch to Victory in Tunisia* (Wiley, 2002)
Kesselring, Albert *The Memoirs of Field Marshal Kesselring* (Morrow, 1953)
Knickerbocker, H.R. et. al. *Danger Forward: The Story of the First Division in World War II* (Battery Press, 2002)
Knox, Macgregor *Hitler's Italian Allies* (Cambridge, 2000)
Lavoie, Leon et al. *American Armor at Faïd–Kasserine* (US Army Armor School, 1949)
Piekalkiewicz, Janusz *Rommel and the Secret War in North Africa 1941–43* (Schiffer, 1992)
Robinett, Paul *Armor Command* (MacGregor, 1958)
Rolf, David *The Bloody Road to Tunis* (Greenhill, 2001)
US Army Historical Division, *To Bizerte with the II Corps* (War Department, 1943)
Watson, Bruce *Exit Rommel: The Tunisian Campaign 1942–43* (Praeger, 1999)

INDEX

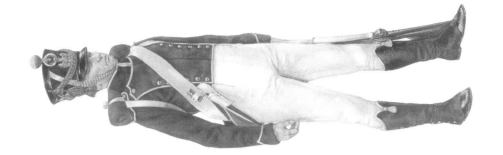 

FIND OUT MORE ABOUT OSPREY

❏ Please send me the latest listing of Osprey's publications

❏ I would like to subscribe to Osprey's e-mail newsletter

Title / rank

Name

Address

City / county

Postcode / zip   state / country

e-mail

CAM

I am interested in:

❏ Ancient world
❏ Medieval world
❏ 16th century
❏ 17th century
❏ 18th century
❏ Napoleonic
❏ 19th century

❏ American Civil War
❏ World War 1
❏ World War 2
❏ Modern warfare
❏ Military aviation
❏ Naval warfare

Please send to:

North America:
Osprey Direct, c/o Random House Distribution Center,
400 Hahn Road, Westminster, MD 21157, USA

UK, Europe and rest of world:
Osprey Direct UK, P.O. Box 140, Wellingborough,
Northants, NN8 2FA, United Kingdom

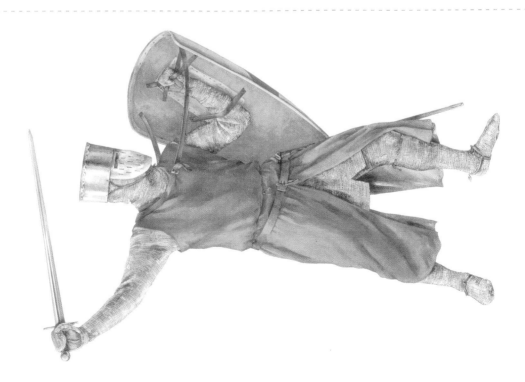

OSPREY
PUBLISHING

Young Guardsman
Figure taken from Warrior 22:
Imperial Guardsman 1799–1815
Published by Osprey
Illustrated by Richard Hook

www.ospreypublishing.com

Knight, c.1190
Figure taken from Warrior 1: Norman Knight 950 - 1204 AD
Published by Osprey
Illustrated by Christa Hook

POSTCARD